Pragmatism and Educational Research

Philosophy, Theory, and Educational Research
Nicholas C. Burbules, Series Editor

Books forthcoming in this series:

Cognitivism and Educational Research
by Ralph E. Reynolds and Nicholas C. Burbules

Poststructuralism and Educational Research
by Michael Peters and Nicholas C. Burbules

Feminism and Educational Research
by Wendy R. Kohli and Nicholas C. Burbules

Pragmatism and Educational Research

By Gert J. J. Biesta and
Nicholas C. Burbules

ROWMAN & LITTLEFIELD PUBLISHERS, INC.
Lanham • Boulder • New York • Toronto • Oxford

ROWMAN & LITTLEFIELD PUBLISHERS, INC.

Published in the United States of America
by Rowman & Littlefield Publishers, Inc.
A wholly owned subsidiary of The Rowman & Littlefield Publishing Group, Inc.
4501 Forbes Boulevard, Suite 200, Lanham, MD 20706
www.rowmanlittlefield.com

P.O. Box 317, Oxford OX2 9RU, UK

British Library Cataloguing in Publication Information Available

Library of Congress Cataloging-in-Publication Data

Biesta, Gert.
  Pragmatism and educational research / by Gert J.J. Biesta and Nicholas
C. Burbules.
    p. cm. — (Philosophy, theory, and educational research)
Includes bibliographical references and index.
  ISBN 0-8476-9476-3 (cloth : alk. paper) — ISBN 0-8476-9477-1 (pbk. :
alk. paper)
  1. Education—Philosophy. 2. Pragmatism. 3. Dewey, John, 1859-1952—
Contributions in education. 4. Education—Research—Methodology.
I. Burbules, Nicholas C. II. Title. III. Series

  LB14.7.B53 2003
  370'.1—dc21

                                                                  2003011857

Printed in the United States of America

∞™ The paper used in this publication meets the minimum requirements of American
National Standard for Information Sciences—Permanence of Paper for Printed Library
Materials, ANSI/NISO Z39.48-1992.

Contents

Series Preface

This book with Gert Biesta is the second in a series appearing with Rowman & Littlefield Publishers: "Philosophy, Theory, and Educational Research." Contemporary educational research has been experiencing an explosion of new methodologies and approaches to inquiry. Many of these approaches have drawn from philosophical or theoretical positions that underlie their determinations of research methods, aims, and criteria of validity. Yet the substance of these philosophical or theoretical assumptions is not always made clear to the reader, and so it is difficult for one to judge those assumptions for oneself.

This series is designed to explore some of the dominant philosophical and theoretical positions influencing educational research today, in a manner that does justice to the substance of these views and shows their relevance for research aims and practices. Each volume will show how a particular set of philosophical and theoretical positions affects the methods and aims of educational research and each will discuss specific examples of research that show these orientations at work. The emphasis is on lively, accessible, but theoretically sound explorations of the issues. These books are intended to be of interest not only to educational researchers but to anyone in education wanting to understand what these various "isms" are about.

This series features a distinguished international group of scholars. It is important for the reader to know that the first author of each volume has been primarily responsible for conceptualizing and drafting the text. The series editor has played a very active role in selecting the topics and the organization for each volume, has interacted regularly with the first author as the text has been drafted, and has had a relatively free hand in revising the text and adding or suggesting new material. This is a more involved role than editors normally play, so second authorship seemed the appropriate appellation. However, the predominant voice and point of view for each volume in the series belongs to the first author. It could not be otherwise, since no coauthor could equally advocate all the positions, many of them mutually inconsistent, argued in these volumes.

1

What Is Pragmatism?

No conclusion of scientific research can be converted into an immediate rule of educational art.

—John Dewey (1929b, 9)

It is widely expected that educational research should generate knowledge that is relevant for the day-to-day practice of educators. Educators do not simply want to know how the world "out there" is. They want knowledge that can inform their actions and activities. The same is true for educational policymakers and politicians. They also seek knowledge that can support and guide their decision making. Educational research, one might say, is not so much research *about* education as it is research *for* education.

The idea that educational research should be relevant for educational practice is far from new. Ever since the end of the eighteenth century, when education became the object of systematic scientific inquiry, educationists have stressed the practical orientation and significance of educational research. This was a central concern for authors like Johann Heinrich Pestalozzi, Johann Friedrich Herbart, and Friedrich Schleiermacher, the founding fathers of modern educational theory. It has become even more important today, at a time when educational researchers are continuously confronted with questions about the practical meaning and relevance of their work.

Although there is almost unanimous agreement about the idea that educational research should have a practical orientation, there are many different views about *the way* in which educational research should play its practical role. Some argue, for example, that educational research should provide educators with educational techniques. On this account, the task of educators becomes one of implementing general educational "truths" that are produced elsewhere. Others maintain that educational research provides different interpretations of educational reality. Practitioners can use these interpretations to understand and make sense of the educational situations they are in.

The way in which the relationship of educational research and educational practice is seen has everything to do with beliefs about knowledge, reality, and human action. If one assumes, for example, that knowledge can provide us with information about reality as it "really" is, and if one further assumes that there is only one reality, then one might conclude that there is eventually only one right way to act. If, on the other hand, one believes that the world of human action is created through action and interaction, and that knowledge is intimately connected with what people do, then new knowledge opens up new and unforeseen possibilities, rather than telling us the one and only possible way to act.

These observations indicate that questions about the relationship between educational research and educational practice immediately raise wider philosophical questions about knowledge, reality, and human action. This should already be sufficient to persuade those who are involved in educational research—either as "producers" or as "users" of research—of the value of engaging in philosophical reflection. But this should not be done for its own sake. We want to argue that philosophical reflection is needed first and foremost because it can help us unravel questions about the *ownership* of knowledge and about the *authority* of educational research and educational researchers in relation to the judgments of educational practitioners.

We do not want to claim that the philosophical tradition that forms the substance of this book—pragmatism—has given final answers to these questions. But we do want to argue that pragmatist philosophers dealt with these issues in a new and unprecedented way and that pragmatism is as relevant today as it was more than a century ago, when the pragmatists began to criticize the disconnected and dehumanized way in which Western culture had for more than two thousand years conceived of knowledge and reality.

It is the purpose of this book to make clear where pragmatism is situated in the history of Western philosophy, what its views about knowledge, reality, and human action are, and how these views might be relevant for our understanding of and approach to educational research today, both from the point of view of those who conduct educational research and from the point of view of those who use, or are affected by, its outcomes. This book is less about designing and recommending a specifically "pragmatist" style of educational research, although we offer some suggestions along those lines, and more about how practitioners of various research approaches might rethink their methods and purposes from within a pragmatist outlook.

Although we pay attention to the wider philosophical movement called "pragmatism," our primary focus in this book is on the ideas of John Dewey (1859–1952). This is not only because Dewey was a world-renowned educator and philosopher. It is also because Dewey wrote extensively and in detail about the process of (scientific) inquiry and its relationship to human action. Most of all, it is because we believe that many of Dewey's ideas are still relevant today—something that, despite the many books that have been written about Dewey over the past two decades, has not yet sufficiently been recognized, at least in the context of educational research.

In this chapter our main aim is to make clear what pragmatism is and how we should understand its place in the history of modern philosophy. The explanations in this chapter provide the background for more detailed discussions about knowledge, action, and educational research in the subsequent chapters of this book.

WHAT IS PRAGMATISM?

We will answer this question in two steps: First we look at the history of pragmatism as a general movement, and then we provide a more systematic presentation of some of the key ideas and key assumptions of Deweyan pragmatism.

A Historical Answer

The Origins of Pragmatism

Pragmatism can be defined as a school of thought that emerged primarily from the writings of three American thinkers: the natural scientist and philosopher Charles Sanders Peirce (1839–1914), the psychologist and philosopher William James (1842–1910), and the philosopher, psychologist, and educationalist John Dewey (1859–1952). Peirce, James, and Dewey are usually seen as the founding fathers of pragmatism. The social psychologist and philosopher George Herbert Mead (1863–1931) contributed much to the further development of pragmatism (Cook 1993; Biesta 1998), and the philosopher Clarence Irving Lewis (1883–1964), although of a younger generation, is sometimes included as another key pragmatist (Thayer 1973).

It has often been argued that pragmatism was the first truly *American* philosophical movement. Although in some ways pragmatism does reflect a distinctly American outlook on the world (Burbules et al., forthcoming), some qualifying remarks must be made. First of all it should be stressed that there is not one pragmatism but many. Not only did the pragmatists cover a wide range of different philosophical topics—from logic, methodology, and metaphysics to ethics, politics, and education—there are also important differences among their ideas. Peirce's dissatisfaction with James's individualistic approach, to name the most salient example, eventually even led him to rename his version of pragmatism "*pragmaticism*"—a name Peirce thought was "ugly enough to be safe from kidnappers" (Peirce 1955, 255).

Second, pragmatism has often been characterized as the philosophical expression of a "typical" American mentality, exemplified in such alleged traits as a pioneering spirit, an urge for expansion, a commercial attitude, and a lack of historical consciousness. Not only does this characterization rely on a rather superficial understanding of North American culture and of the interaction between culture and philosophy more generally, more to the point, it does no justice at all to the philosophical depth of pragmatism. Dewey's response to Bertrand Russell's suggestion that pragmatism was the philosophical expression of American commercialism (Russell 1922) says it well:

"The suggestion that pragmatism is the intellectual equivalent of commercialism . . . is of that order of interpretation which would say that English neo-realism is a reflection of the aristocratic snobbery of the English; the tendency of French thought to dualism an expression of an alleged Gallic disposition to keep a mistress in addition to a wife; and the idealism of Germany a manifestation of an ability to elevate beer and sausage into a higher synthesis with the spiritual values of Beethoven and Wagner." (Dewey 1922a, 307)

All this is not to deny that pragmatism was the first philosophical "school" to emerge in North America. Pragmatism can be seen as the first original contribution to an intellectual tradition that was initially dominated by theological thought and, after that, by several varieties of British empiricism (particularly Locke and Berkeley) and German idealism (particularly Hegel and Schelling) (Kuklick 1985; Schneider 1963). Moreover, it is significant that the emergence of pragmatism coincided with the establishment of philosophy as an independent academic discipline at North American universities, since this gave it institutional legitimacy and influence.

The fact that pragmatism emerged in the North American context does not mean, however, that it was exclusively composed of North American material. The pragmatists were all deeply influenced by European philosophy. Peirce had an intimate knowledge of Immanuel Kant's work. In an autobiographical essay he disclosed that he studied Kant's *Critique of Pure Reason* for two hours a day for more than three years until he "almost knew the whole book by heart" (Peirce 1955, 2). Dewey, whose (lost) dissertation was on Kant, began his philosophical career as a devout follower of Hegel, and although he eventually developed his own version of pragmatism, the acquaintance with Hegel left a "permanent deposit" in his thinking (Dewey 1930b, 154; Welchman 1989). Unlike Peirce and Dewey, James and Mead received a considerable part of their academic education at European (German) universities, something that was quite common in their time.

Although pragmatism is strongly rooted in the Western philosophical tradition, it differs in one very important respect from this tradition, because all pragmatists argued in one way or another that philosophy should take the methods and insights of modern science into account. Dewey, for example, stressed the significance of the experimental method of modern science as a model for human problem solving and the acquisition of knowledge. Peirce, who claimed that he was "saturated, through and through, with the spirit of the physical sciences" (Peirce 1955, 1), even described his philosophy "as the attempt of a physicist to make such conjecture as to the constitution of the universe as the methods of science may permit, with the aid of all that has been done by previous philosophers" (Peirce 1955, 2).

This approach led Peirce to an understanding of the meaning of concepts in strictly experimentalist terms. In a seminal essay from 1878, entitled "How to make our ideas clear," Peirce stated the central idea of his theory in the following way: "Consider what effects, that might conceivably have practical bearings, we conceive the object of our conception to have. Then, our conception of these effects is the whole of our conception of the object" (1955, 31).

On the basis of this theory, Peirce argued that when we call a thing *hard* this means nothing more than that it will not be scratched by many other substances. He also claimed that since the whole conception of this quality lies in its conceived effects, there is no difference between a hard thing and a soft thing *so long as they are not brought to the test*, so long, that is, if we don't do anything with them. "[D]ifferent beliefs are distinguished by the different modes of action to which they give rise. If beliefs do not differ in this respect . . . then no mere differences in the manner of consciousness of them can make them different beliefs" (1955, 29).

This experimentalist theory of the meaning of concepts asserted an intimate connection between knowledge and action. Peirce argued that in order to attribute meaning to concepts one must be able to apply them to existence. Kant had referred to the situation in which knowledge and action are strictly separate as "practical" and the situation in which knowledge and action are intimately connected as "pragmatic." It was for this reason that Peirce (initially) decided to name his philosophy *pragmatism* — and not practicism or practicalism (Peirce 1955, 252; Dewey 1925b, 3).

The Contemporary Context

During the larger part of the twentieth century, pragmatism occupied a rather marginal position in the Western philosophical tradition. On the European continent the philosophical scene was dominated by phenomenology (Edmund Husserl, Martin Heidegger, Maurice Merleau-Ponty), existentialism (Jean-Paul Sartre) and neo-Marxism (Max Horkheimer, Theodor W. Adorno, Herbert Marcuse, Jürgen Habermas). In the Anglo-Saxon world, analytic philosophy reigned strong. The writings on logic and language by analytic philosophers such as Gottlob Frege, Bertrand Russell, Alfred North Whitehead, and Ludwig Wittgenstein were an important point of reference for the members of the *Wiener Kreis* (the "Vienna Circle," among them Moritz Schlick, Rudolf Carnap, and Otto Neurath), a group of philosophers of science working together in Vienna before World War II. Shortly before the war, several members of this group fled to the United States, as a result of which analytic philosophy rapidly gained prominence in North America. Through the writings of philosophers such as Hans Reichenbach, Carl Hempel, Ernest Nagel, and Karl Popper, analytic philosophy, for a long time, dominated the face of modern philosophy of science.

The situation for pragmatism changed dramatically as a result of two developments. On the one hand, several American philosophers who worked in the analytic tradition came to the conclusion that the fundamental assumptions of that tradition were no longer tenable. Their critique of analytic philosophy led them to a rediscovery of some of the key ideas of pragmatism.

In 1951 Willard van Orman Quine published a groundbreaking article called "The Two Dogmas of Empiricism" (Quine 1980, 20–46), in which he claimed that it was impossible to make a fundamental distinction between truths that are analytic, that is grounded in meanings independent of matters of fact (like "all bachelors are unmarried"), and truths that are synthetic, or grounded in fact (like "the earth revolves around the sun"). He argued that analytic truths, such as the truths of logic and mathematics, can in principle be modified and even abandoned in the light of experience, just as we do with our factual statements. Quine thereby refuted one of the founding assumptions of analytic philosophy, namely, the idea that some propositions—the propositions of logic and mathematics, for example—are true *independent of human experience*.

Quine also criticized the idea of reductionism, that is, the belief that individual statements can be linked to individual experiences and that in this way their truth can be proved. He argued that our statements always hang together in a network, a "web of beliefs." This not only means, according to Quine, that our statements about the external world face the tribunal of sense experience as a corporate body of statements and never individually, it also implies that any statement can be held true if we are willing to make drastic enough changes elsewhere in the system. In terms of research, Quine's point is that observation as such never gives us knowledge; observation only becomes meaningful through interpretation, and when we interpret our observations, a whole body of assumptions and theory comes into play. Quine's critique of reductionism was a direct attack on one of the central ideas of the philosophers of the *Wiener Kreis*, that the "building blocks" for true scientific knowledge were to be found in individual, elementary sense experiences (which is the root idea of all empiricism). Quine labeled his position a "thorough pragmatism" (1980, 46).

Donald Davidson, a student of Quine's, also contributed to the waning of analytic philosophy of science by criticizing a "third dogma" of empiricism, namely, the assumption that it is possible to make a distinction between experience and the conceptual schemes in which we interpret and organize our experience (Davidson 1984, 183–98). Davidson also criticized the idea that the acquisition of knowledge is an individual enterprise and rather stressed the social or intersubjective nature of meaning, knowledge, and thinking (Davidson 1980). The latter point is also central in the work of Hilary Putnam, the analytic philosopher who has most explicitly made the transition to pragmatism (Putnam 1995; 1990).

While on the one hand pragmatism regained status as a result of these internal critiques and reconstructions of the analytic tradition, there were other philosophers who developed a pragmatist critique of analytic philosophy from the "outside." The most important figure here is without doubt the American philosopher Richard Rorty. In 1979 Rorty published *Philosophy and the Mirror of Nature* in which he criticized the preoccupation of modern philosophy with the human mind as a "mirror of nature," and of knowledge as a representation in the mind of the world "outside." Rorty stressed the practical nature of all our knowledge and the indispensable role of language in knowledge and in the acquisition of knowledge. Against this background Rorty argued for a turn from objectivity to solidarity. In his book Rorty called Dewey one of the three most important philosophers of the twentieth century—the other two being Wittgenstein and Heidegger (Rorty 1980, 5). In a later book, *Consequences of Pragmatism* (1982), Rorty even argued that Dewey and James "were not only waiting at the end of the dialectical road which analytic philosophy traveled, but are waiting at the end of the road which for example Foucault and Deleuze are currently traveling" (1982, xviii). For Rorty, then, pragmatism is the culmination of several quite different philosophical movements.

At the beginning of the twenty-first century, in an era that is often termed "*post-analytic*" (Rajchman and West 1985), pragmatism has once again become a philosophical tradition to be reckoned with. This is true for "neo-pragmatists" like Rorty and Richard Bernstein (Bernstein 1983; 1986); it is true for "analytic pragmatists" like Quine, Davidson, and Putnam; and it is true for the "original" pragmatists. In all this, Dewey's work has especially attracted renewed interest (Boydston and Poulos, 1978; http://www.siu.edu/~deweyctr).

A Philosophical Answer

In 1908, Arthur Lovejoy, a fierce critic of pragmatism, published an essay in which he argued that there were at least thirteen different pragmatisms. Lovejoy not only claimed that these pragmatisms were separate in the sense of being discriminable, he also argued that they were logically independent, so that "you may without inconsistency accept any one and reject all the others" (1963, 2). Lovejoy's attempt to define pragmatism—which did not even at that point include Dewey's work—indicates how difficult it already was in the early years of pragmatism to come to a clear definition. One century and many books and articles later, things are not any easier. Hence, the characterization of Dewey's position that we give in this book is not the final word about Dewey, but is just one possible way to understand his work. In this section we present some of the key ideas of Dewey's version of pragmatism, which we will return to again in later chapters. Our guiding question at this point is: What does Dewey's pragmatism have to offer for educational research?

The main significance of Dewey's pragmatism for educational research lies in the fact that it provides a different account of knowledge and a different understanding of the way in which human beings can acquire knowledge. Dewey's approach is different in that he deals with questions of knowledge and the acquisition of knowledge within the framework of a philosophy of *action*, in fact, a philosophy that takes action as its *most basic* category. This connection between knowledge and action is especially relevant for those who approach questions about knowledge primarily from a practical angle—such as educators and educational researchers.

One could say, then, that Dewey provided a new epistemology for educational research. But calling Dewey's ideas about knowledge an *epistemology* is somewhat misleading if—and the "if" is crucial here—one thinks of epistemology as the branch of philosophy that tries to give an answer to the question of how our (immaterial) mind can acquire knowledge of a (material) world outside our mind. One of Dewey's key points is that this question only makes sense if one assumes that the distinction between mind and matter, and between "inside" and "outside," is an original and inevitable distinction, a given for all philosophy. In modern philosophy, since René Descartes (1596–1650), this was indeed assumed to be the case. Descartes argued that reality consisted of two kinds of "stuff": *res extensa*, the "stuff" that occupies space, and *res cogitans*, the mental "stuff" of the human cogito (the knowing mind). If this assumption is the point of departure for all philosophy, then it is indeed crucial to find an answer to the question how that (immaterial) mind can get in touch with a (material) world. Many modern philosophers up to the present time continue to see this as one of the main questions for which philosophy needs to find an answer (for example, Dancy 1985)—and the name for this special branch of philosophy is "*epistemology*."

Perhaps, then, Dewey's different approach ought to be considered an anti-epistemology, because he does not build his understanding of knowledge on this dualism of mind and matter. Instead of the route taken by the "philosophy of consciousness," the philosophy that takes its point of departure in the knowing mind and then asks how this mind can get hold of the world "outside," Dewey took his point of departure in interactions taking place in nature, where nature is itself understood as "a moving whole of interacting parts" (Dewey 1929a, 232). Dewey described this "Copernican turn" in his philosophy as follows: "The old center was mind . . . [t]he new center is indefinite interactions" (1929a, 232). The interactions that are of specific importance for Dewey are the interactions between the living human organism and its environment. Human action, Dewey argued, is always "the *interaction* between elements of human nature and the environment, natural and social" (1922b, 9). The interaction—or as he later would call it *trans*action—of organism and environment is an active, adaptive, and adjustive process in which the organism seeks to maintain a dynamic balance with its ever-changing environment.

One of the most important implications of Dewey's transactional approach is that it tries to account for the *point of contact* between the human organism and the world. For Dewey the human organism is always already "in touch" with reality, unlike the dualistic philosophy of consciousness, which separates the immaterial mind and the material world. But while Dewey's transactional approach implies that the organism is always "in touch" with its environment, this does not mean that reality simply reveals itself to the organism. One of the key ideas of Dewey's pragmatism (consistent with Peirce's theory of meaning) is that reality only "reveals" itself as a result of the activities—the "doings"—of the organism.

Stated in philosophical terms, we can say that Dewey's transactional approach is clearly based on realist assumptions. His philosophy is not "idealistic" in that it does not deny or doubt the existence of a world "outside." Reality is, however, for Dewey only "experienced" (we will come back to the specific meaning of the term "*experience*" for Dewey in chapter 2) as a function of the organism-environment transaction. It is in this sense that Dewey's version of realism might best be referred to as *transactional realism* (Sleeper 1986).

Dewey's transactional realism dissolves many of the questions that have troubled philosophers up to the present day. One of these questions concerns the objectivity of knowledge. Some philosophers argue that true knowledge should be objective, which basically means that it should be an accurate depiction of the objects—the "things"—in the world. Other philosophers argue that knowledge is a human construction, that it is a product of the human mind, and that it is therefore ultimately subjective. Given what we have said so far, it should be clear that both objectivism and subjectivism derive their meaning from the dualistic mind-world scheme. Objectivism argues that knowledge should be completely "of the world." Subjectivism maintains that knowledge is completely of the mind. Although Dewey's transactional realism does assert that knowledge is a construction, it is not a construction of the human mind, but a construction that is located in the organism-environment transaction itself. What is constructed—over and over again—is the dynamic balance of organism and environment, which manifests itself both in specific changes in the environment and specific changes in the patterns of action of the organism. Dewey's transactional realism, in other words, is also a "transactional constructivism" because it can be argued that our knowledge is at the very same time a construction *and* based on reality. In this sense, Dewey's transactional framework provides an approach that goes beyond the traditional distinction between objectivism and relativism. (We will return to this topic in chapter 4.)

At this point we should mention that our use of the word *"knowledge"* in the previous remarks does not necessarily refer to propositional knowledge, that is, to claims about the world that we put explicitly into words. According to Dewey's transactional approach, knowledge manifests itself first of all in the way in which organisms transact with and respond to changes in their environment. This is the import of Dewey's claim that knowledge lives first "in the muscles"—and not in the mind. The fact that we know something reveals itself initially on the level of action and only later in symbolic forms (like language). Through our constant transactions with our environment, through our continuous attempts to maintain a dynamic balance with our environment, we develop patterns of possible action, which Dewey called *habits*. The acquisition of habits, of possible ways to respond to and transact with our environment, is basically a process of trial and error. We do something (and Dewey emphasized that we are always doing something, and cannot *not* do something) that affects our environment, we undergo the consequences of our doings, and try to adjust ourselves accordingly—and this cycle repeats itself. In the act of knowing—and hence in research—both the knower and what is to be known are changed by the transaction between them.

Trial and error is, however, not the only way in which human beings can gain knowledge. Dewey argued that we can escape the immediacy of trial and error by means of the use of symbols. By performing symbolic operations—an activity that Dewey called "*thinking*"—we can try different lines of action without actually being subjected to the consequences of these lines of action. Obviously, this can only help us in considering *possible* lines of action, and in this way it can help us to make our responses more precise or more "intelligent," as Dewey would put it. But it is only when we actually do respond that we can know whether the suggested line of action was appropriate. While the use of symbols can make our decision making more intelligent, the ultimate proof is to be found in the field of action. We must act in order to find out whether a suggested response is indeed appropriate for the situation in which we are engaged.

There is one further aspect of Dewey's position that we want to mention in this initial outline of his ideas. It could well be argued that Dewey's transactional constructivism ultimately implies that we each construct our own, individual world. And indeed in one sense this is the case. We all live in our own world, a world that is meaningful for us in a way that it can't be meaningful for anybody else. Dewey argued, however, that when individuals act together in order to achieve a common goal, they need to adjust their individual approaches, their individual perspectives and patterns of action in such a way that a coordinated response becomes possible. In this process their individual worlds are transformed. These worlds do not become identical, but what does happen, Dewey argued, is that the partners in interaction create a shared, *intersubjective*, world. They make, in other words, "something in common"—and it is for precisely this reason that Dewey referred to this process as *communication*. Communication is not the simple transfer of information from one mind to another, but the practical coordination and reconstruction of individual patterns of action, which results in the creation of a shared, intersubjective world. Since this intersubjective world is created through action—and not through the transfer of information from one mind to another—we suggest calling this dimension of Dewey's work "practical intersubjectivity" (Biesta 1994).

This should suffice as a first outline of Dewey's pragmatist theory of knowledge, which, as we have argued, is *not* an *epistemology* in the traditional sense of the word. The two main and most distinctive components of Dewey's position are his *transactional realism* and his idea of communication as *practical intersubjectivity*. On a more general level, we have tried to make clear how Dewey's philosophy can be seen as a critique of the tradition of the "philosophy of consciousness," that is, the tradition that assumes that the first reality for all philosophy is consciousness. Such a point of departure leads to difficult if not impossible questions, such as how this disconnected consciousness can ever get in touch with reality. This question simply disappears in Dewey's transactional approach, in which it is assumed that we are constantly "in transaction" with the world. One of the interesting implications of this point of departure is that it allows Dewey to move beyond the traditional opposition of objectivism and subjectivism. It also allows Dewey to combine constructivism and realism.

One could argue that Dewey's theory of knowledge is a form of *fallibilism*, because it follows from his account that we can never be completely certain about our knowledge. This fundamental uncertainty is, however, not the product of an alleged gap between mind and matter or consciousness and reality. For Dewey the uncertainty of knowledge stems from the fact that we can never be certain that the patterns of action that we have developed in the past will be appropriate for the problems that we will encounter in the future. Dewey's fallibilism is, in other words, *practical* and not structural. It has to do with the fact that we live in an ever-changing world in which each new situation is in some respect unique. The ways in which the world can surprise us always provide input into the cycle of inquiry and action, forcing us to change our knowledge of the world and our ways of acting within it (which, in turn, can yield new experiences to learn from).

While this overview gives a first understanding of some of the most central ideas of Dewey's philosophy, it is important to keep in mind that the reason why Dewey invested so much time and energy in the development of a new understanding of knowledge was not primarily because he wanted to develop a new contribution to philosophy, but because he thought that the development of such a theory was crucial for addressing some of the most profound problems of modern life. Dewey was convinced that philosophy should not be occupied solely with the problems of philosophers but that it should be a method, cultivated by philosophers, to deal with the "problems of men [*sic*]" (Dewey 1917, 46). In order to be able to appreciate the larger significance of Dewey's ideas about knowledge and action, we need to say a bit more about Dewey's more general "project."

THE PROJECT OF PRAGMATISM

Was Dewey a Positivist?

In his book *Reconstruction in Philosophy* Dewey observed that "intelligent method, logic, is still far to seek in moral and political affairs" (1920, 159). Against this background he argues "for the adoption in moral reflection of the logic that has been proved to make for security, stringency and fertility in passing judgments upon physical phenomena" (1920, 174). Some have taken Dewey's plea for a "scientific treatment of morality" (1903a, 3–39) and his endorsement of the method of the natural sciences to mean that he was a positivist, that is, someone who holds the view that we should only rely upon "positive" knowledge (knowledge firmly rooted in reality), and not upon "speculative" knowledge (the knowledge of, for example, theology and philosophy). Others have accused Dewey of "scientism," which is the view that what the natural sciences have to say about the world is all there is to say. For example, Max Horkheimer, a German neo-Marxist philosopher, has argued that Dewey's "worship of natural sciences" made it impossible for him to take a critical stance (Horkheimer, 1947, 46–49).

Dewey was very clear about the value and importance of what he commonly refers to as the "scientific method," because "its comparative maturity as a form of knowledge exemplifies so conspicuously the necessary place and function of experimentation" (1939b, 12). But he hastens to add that his appreciation for the *method* of the natural sciences "would be misinterpreted if it were taken to mean that science is the only valid kind of knowledge" (1929a, 200). Rather, scientific method has proven its value through its practical successes in experimentation and problem solving. This is all that recommends it, not that science is a privileged avenue to the Truth in any fundamental sense. Furthermore, Dewey not only rejected the idea that the knowledge provided by the natural sciences is the only valid kind of knowledge, he even argued against the more general idea that *knowledge* is the only way in which we can get in touch with reality.

If there is one recurring theme in Dewey's work, it is precisely his critique of the idea that knowledge is the "measure of the reality of [all] other modes of experience" (1929a, 235).

The main problem of the identification of what is known with what is real, is that it makes it appear as if all the other dimensions of human life—such as the practical, the aesthetic, the ethical, or the religious dimensions—can only be real if they can be reduced to and validated by what is revealed through our knowledge. In such a view, love is only considered to be real if it can be explained in terms of hormones, knowledge is only real if it can be traced back to events in our brains, and compassion is only real if it can be found to exist in our genes. By assuming that knowledge provides the "norm" for what is real, other aspects of the ways in which humans live their lives and are "in the world" are relegated to the domain of the subjective—the domain of individual taste, points of view, feelings, and individual perspectives. Dewey described the problem as follows: "When real objects are identified . . . with knowledge-objects, all affectional and volitional objects are inevitably excluded from the 'real' world, and are compelled to find refuge in the privacy of an experiencing subject or mind" (1925a, 30). The identification of what is known with what is real has, in other words, driven a wedge between people and their many ways of being in and interacting with the world. Those aspects of human life that make it most typically human have been denied reality and, as a result of this, have been denied rationality. The identification of what is known with what is real has made the human actor into an "unnaturalized and unnaturalizable alien in the world" (Dewey 1925a, 30).

Dewey believed that the identification of what is known with what is real was one of the most fundamental mistakes of modern philosophy, a mistake that he referred to as the "intellectualist fallacy" (1929a, 175; 1925a, 28–30). One way to understand Dewey's project, then, is to see it as an attempt to undo this mistake so that those dimensions of our being in the world that cannot be traced back to (scientific) knowledge can again be seen as real and rational.

In order to do this, Dewey had to make clear that the domain of knowledge and the domain of human action are not separate domains, but are intimately connected: that knowledge emerges from action and feeds back into action, and that it does not have a separate existence or function. The reason why Dewey turned to modern science to make this point is precisely because the experimental approach of modern natural science is one in which knowledge and action *are already* intimately and inextricably

connected. For those who think that introducing the idea of action into the
domain of knowledge poses a threat to the purity, truth, and objectivity of
scientific knowledge, this may come as a shock. Dewey simply argued,
however, that such assumptions about (scientific) knowledge rely on an
epistemology that was developed long before the emergence of the experimental method of modern science—an epistemology, moreover, that
bears no resemblance to how science actually yields knowledge.

Dewey took this line of thought even further when he argued that the
experimental approach of the natural sciences actually looks much more
like the style of reasoning and judgment that is commonly reserved for the
domain of value, in that it is fallible, focused on individual cases, and intimately connected with action. He therefore wrote, "The actual point of
my theory may . . . be found in the transfer of traits which has been reserved for the function of moral judgment over to the processes of ordinary and scientific knowledge" (1939b, 62).

That this is anything but a positivistic strategy becomes still more clear
in the following statement from Dewey's 1903 article "The Logical Conditions of a Scientific Treatment of Morality":

> "[T]here is no question of eliminating the distinctive quality of ethical
> judgments by assimilating them to a different logical type found in so-called
> scientific judgments; precisely because the logical type found in recognized
> scientific judgments is one which already takes due account of individual-
> ization and activity." (1903a, 8)

This quote makes clear why Dewey was not a positivist and cannot be accused of scientism. When he argued for the adoption of the method of modern science in other domains of life, he is not talking about this method as
one that can provide absolute certainty. For him the scientific method stands
for an experimental, fallibilist approach in which knowledge and action are
inextricably connected. Part of what Dewey wanted to achieve was the development of a theory of knowledge that is consistent with the actual experimental method of modern science. But it is important to see that Dewey did
not simply want to develop a more up-to-date understanding of knowledge
and the acquisition of knowledge. Behind this work lies a much more encompassing concern—to which we turn now.

The Crisis in Culture

Dewey saw his work as a response to a "crisis" in modern culture. The
central element in this crisis, according to Dewey, is the disintegrating

influence of modern science on everyday life—or, with the phrase Dewey preferred, "common sense" (1948, 265; 1929a, 32–33). Modern science has completely changed our understanding of the world in which we live. It has given us a view of the world as a mechanism, as "a scene of indifferent physical particles acting according to mathematical and mechanical laws." Modern science "has stripped the world of the qualities which made it beautiful and congenial to men [*sic*]" (Dewey 1929a, 33). Dewey argued that the disintegrative influence of this development on "common sense" is mainly caused by the way in which the scientific worldview has been *interpreted*, namely, as an account of reality as it "really" is. As we have already seen, this view has resulted in a derogation of the reality of the world of everyday experience and of the reality of the noncognitive dimensions of human life:

> The net practical effect is the creation of the belief that science exists only in the things which are most remote from any significant human concern, so that as we approach social and moral questions and interests we must either surrender hope of the guidance of genuine knowledge or else purchase scientific title and authority at the expense of all that is distinctly human." (1939b, 51)

The problem is, in other words, that the realistic interpretation of the mechanistic worldview has put us in a situation with two, equally unattractive options: the *inhuman rationality* of modern science or the *human irrationality* of common sense. It is this predicament that lies at the heart of the crisis in culture—which reveals that this crisis is first and foremost *a crisis of rationality*.

The fact that Dewey relates the crisis in culture to a specific interpretation of the mechanistic worldview should not be read to imply that the crisis is only a theoretical problem and has, therefore, nothing to do with the urgent practical problems of contemporary society. Dewey rather wants to stress that the hegemony of scientific reality and scientific rationality—that is, the situation in which it is assumed that rationality only has to do with the "hard facts" of science, and not with values, morals, feelings, emotions, and so on—makes it almost impossible to find an adequate solution for these problems, since the situation we are in is one in which rationality gets restricted to facts and means, while values and ends are, by definition, excluded from rational deliberation. This is why we call the crisis in culture a crisis of rationality.

What makes this problem even more urgent, Dewey argued, is the fact that to a large extent modern life is what it is as a result of the "embodiment of science in the common sense world" (1938a, 81). We are, therefore, constantly confronted by the products and effects of modern science: cars, computers, hospitals. It is for this reason that the dilemma of inhuman rationality versus human irrationality is felt most deeply in the sphere of "common sense," in the sphere of our everyday lives. This is why Dewey wrote that the "outstanding problem of our civilization" is set by the fact "that common sense in its content, its 'world' and methods is a house divided against itself" (1938a, 84). Is it possible to overcome this division? Dewey thought that philosophy must at least try to do so: "The problem of restoring integration and co-operation between man's [*sic*] beliefs about the world in which he lives and his beliefs about values and purposes that should direct his conduct is the deepest problem of any philosophy that is not isolated from that life" (1939b, 8–9).

In order to achieve integration, two philosophical problems must be solved (Dewey 1939b, 8–9). First of all, we need to find out whether it is possible to accept the findings of modern science in such a way that it no longer poses a threat to the realm of *values*, using that word to designate "whatever is taken to have rightful authority in the direction of conduct" (Dewey 1929a, 315). Second, we need to find an answer to the question of whether the world of natural science and the world of everyday life can be reconciled.

Dewey believed that philosophy can help find a way out of the crisis in culture, because philosophy has played such a central role in creating the problem in the first place. The crisis in culture was, after all, the result of a specific interpretation of the findings of modern science, namely, an interpretation that claimed that the knowledge of modern science shows us the world as it really is. In order to understand where this interpretation came from and how it has affected the course of modern philosophy, Dewey went back to the roots of Western philosophy.

A (Very) Brief History of Western Philosophy

Dewey argued that Western philosophy emerged in a society—Greek society—in which knowing was much more valued than doing, and in which theory had a much higher status than practice (Dewey 1916a, 271–85). The reason for this hierarchy was a longing for absolute, immutable certainty, and the recognition that such certainty could not be found in the domain of action (Dewey 1929a, 5–6). The identification of what is absolutely certain with what is immutable led philosophers such as Plato to a *metaphysics*, a philosophy about reality, in which it was maintained that only what is fixed, immutable, and unchangeable can be real, and to an *epistemology* in which it was argued that certain knowledge "must relate to that which has antecedent existence or essential being" (Dewey 1929a, 18). One implication of these assumptions is that true knowledge can only be acquired if the *process of acquiring* knowledge does not exert any influence on the *object* of knowledge (Dewey 1929a, 19). For this reason the process of the acquisition of knowledge was cut off from action and was understood in terms of visual perception—a theory that Dewey called the "spectator theory of knowledge" (1929a, 19): "[T]he notion which has ruled philosophy ever since the time of the Greeks, [is] that the office of knowledge is to uncover the antecedently real, rather than, as is the case with our practical judgments, to gain the kind of understanding which is necessary to deal with the problems as they arise" (1929a, 14). Such ideas deepened the gap between theory and practice. According to this view, theory has to find out how reality *is*. Although practical action is based on the knowledge provided by theory, it is completely disconnected from its acquisition. Practice is "a mere external follower upon knowledge, having no part in its determination. . . . [I]t is supposed to conform to what is fixed in the antecedent structure of things" (1929a, 58).

One of the interesting aspects of the Greek worldview was an assumption that values *were* part of the world. The Greeks assumed, in other words, that reality was purposeful. Everything strives to become what it has in potential: An acorn strives to become an oak tree; a human being strives to become rational. This meant that true, objective knowledge about reality would at the very same time provide guidelines for the direction of human action.

It is not too difficult to see the kind of problems that arose when the mechanical worldview of modern science, the worldview of Copernicus, Galileo, and Newton, emerged. Until then, it had been possible to derive aims and values from the knowledge of reality. But with the emergence of the scientific worldview "science ceased to disclose in the objects of knowledge the possession of any such properties" (1929a, 34). This led to the question of how the results of the new science could be accepted and the domain of values maintained (1929a, 33). Dewey argued that, given the available philosophical framework, there was only one possible solution—that values had to be relegated to a separate domain: "Qualities, excellencies and ends that were extruded from nature by the new science,"

Dewey wrote, "found their exclusive abode and warrant in the realm of the spiritual" (1929a, 23).

This resulted in the fundamental distinction between the domain of nature and the domain of values (a distinction still with us, for example, in the dictum that "the *is* must be separate from the *ought*"). In order to safeguard the domain of values, it further had to be shown that this domain was superior to the domain of factual knowledge about nature. According to Dewey, this is precisely what Descartes and Kant tried to do—argue that the possibility of scientific knowledge has its ultimate foundation in an immaterial human mind (Dewey 1929a, 33–34). As a result, Dewey wrote, the "opposition and yet necessary connection of nature and spirit" (1929a, 43) became part of what was conceived to be the nature of human beings themselves. It resulted in the dualistic worldview of the material and the spiritual, and in the assumption that the material constitutes "outer" nature, while the spiritual is the realm of "inner" mind.

Dewey's main point in his reading of the development of Western philosophy was to make clear that the distinction between mind and matter, between the subjective and the objective, and between facts and values is not the inevitable or necessary point of departure for all philosophy. It rather was a particular solution that the inaugurators of modern philosophy came up with to tackle the problem of accepting the conclusions of modern science while at the same time maintaining the realm of values. What Dewey's reconstruction also makes clear is that this problem was, in a sense, an artificial problem from the very start, since it was the product of assumptions inherited from Greek philosophy: "If men [*sic*] had associated their ideas about values with practical activity instead of with cognition or antecedent Being," Dewey argued, "they would *not* have been troubled by the findings of science" (Dewey 1929a, 34).

When, against this background, Dewey looks favorably at modern science, it is to emphasize that modern science has not only given us a different view about reality, but that this view has been brought about by an approach—the experimental method—in which the division between knowing and acting has completely disappeared (Dewey 1938a, 80; Dewey 1920). In practice, modern science was therefore from its very inception already in contradiction with the spectator theory of knowledge. Twentieth-century physics was a final blow against Greek metaphysics. In the worldview that emerged in the fifteenth and sixteenth centuries, it was assumed that space and time existed independently of each other and that events took place *in* space and time: "Since the assumption of underlying fixities—of which the matter of space and time and of immutable atoms is an exemplification—dominated 'natural' science, there is no ground for surprise that in a more generalized form it was the foundation upon which philosophy assumed, as a matter of course, that it must erect its structure" (Dewey 1948, 260). But more recent developments in natural science have subverted the idea that reality itself eventually consists of immutable entities or particles: "[T]here recently entered the discovery that natural science is forced by its own development to abandon the assumption of fixity and to recognize that what for it is actually 'universal' is 'process'" (Dewey 1948, 260).

The Quest for Human Rationality

What conclusions can be drawn from this brief survey? As we have seen, Dewey argued that the crisis in culture—which is a crisis of rationality— was an effect of the way in which the mechanistic worldview of modern science was *interpreted*, namely, as an account of what reality "really" is. It is this specific interpretation that has brought about the crisis of rationality, the situation of the two equally unattractive options of inhuman rationality and human irrationality. Dewey's reconstruction of the development of Western philosophy shows that this problem was caused by the fact that the findings of modern science were mistakenly characterized in terms of philosophical categories and dualities that were developed long before the emergence of modern science, in a completely different context and for totally different purposes.

When modern science gained prominence there were, in principle, two options for philosophy. The one that was chosen was to use the existing philosophical framework to make sense of the findings of modern science. This created the problem of how these findings could be accepted while still maintaining the realm of values. The attempt to solve this problem eventually led to the dualistic assumptions that lie at the basis of modern philosophy. Dewey's reconstruction makes clear, however, that these assumptions are just one possible answer to the problems that arose with the emergence of modern science. Dewey's reconstruction suggests that there is another option. Instead of using the Greek framework to interpret the emergence of modern science, philosophers could also have asked what would follow if we would amend our understanding of knowledge and reality according to the findings and methods of modern science itself—which Dewey believed demonstrated the *inseparability* of knowledge and action, fact and value. But, to repeat in conclusion, his reason for exploring this road was not simply to come up with a more adequate theory of knowledge, but to overcome the dilemma of inhuman rationality versus human irrationality. This is a quest, in other words, for a new and different understanding of *human rationality*, a theme that ultimately motivates all of Dewey's writings.

CONCLUSION

In this chapter we have tried to provide an initial answer to the question of what pragmatism is. We have focused mainly on John Dewey, not only because he is the most "educational" of the pragmatists, but also because we believe that his understanding of knowledge and action is most appropriate and relevant for the problems of contemporary educational research. We have argued that Dewey's positive evaluation of the scientific method should not be taken to mean that Dewey was a positivist or that his philosophy is a form of scientism. On the contrary, the whole point of Dewey's philosophy is to overcome the idea that rationality only has to do with questions about the most effective means for bringing about predetermined ends. Dewey wanted to restore reality *and* rationality to the broad spectrum of human concerns. For Dewey, rationality is about intelligent human action and human cooperation. The reason why we have paid so much attention to the wider framework of Dewey's philosophy, therefore, is because we wanted to make clear that not only does Dewey provide us with a new way to think about knowing and acting, but that this philosophical account is ultimately motivated by an attempt to restore rationality, agency, and responsibility to the sphere of human action. We believe that this perspective is of crucial importance for education and educational research today, because education is also not simply a technical enterprise where educators simply "apply" the findings of educational research. Education is a thoroughly human practice in which questions about "how" are inseparable from questions about "why" and "what for."

In the chapters that follow we look at Dewey's ideas about knowledge, action, and inquiry in more detail. In chapter 2 we examine the basic structure of Dewey's "transactionalism" and the ensuing philosophy of action, which together provide the framework for Dewey's theory of knowledge. In chapter 3 we focus on Dewey's theory of inquiry, with special attention to his ideas about inquiry in the social domain, including specifically educational inquiry. In chapter 4 we deal with questions about the relationship between theory and practice, with Dewey's realism, and with questions about objectivism, relativism, and Dewey's "third way." In chapter 5 we present our conclusions about pragmatism and educational research.

2

From Experience to Knowledge

Things are objects to be treated, used, acted upon and with, enjoyed and endured, even more than things to be known. They are things *had* before they are things *cognized.*

—John Dewey (1925a, 28)

We do not have to go to knowledge to obtain an exclusive hold on reality. The world as we experience it is the real world.

—John Dewey (1929a, 235)

As we discussed in chapter 1, Dewey argued that the dualism between mind and world is not the inevitable point of departure for all philosophy but a specific solution for problems that philosophers thought they were faced with when the mechanistic worldview of modern science emerged. This conclusion opens up the possibility for exploring a different approach, one that does not start from the dualism between mind and world but that "contains them both in an unanalyzed totality" (Dewey 1925a, 18). In 1925 Dewey referred to this approach as the "empirical method." Eventually he called it the *transactional approach* (Dewey and Bentley 1949, 127–30).

On the one hand, this approach is presented as a *procedure* or *method* "in which is asserted the right to see together, extensionally and durationally, much that is talked about conventionally as if it were composed of irreconcilable separates" (Dewey and Bentley 1949, 67). Dewey stressed that this monistic strategy doesn't dissolve questions about knowledge. But it does lead to a *different* question—a question that stands a better chance of getting a meaningful answer than the questions of the dualistic philosopher of knowledge. By separating subject and object, mind and matter, and assuming that knowing is a process that occurs outside of nature, the dualistic philosopher of knowledge is faced with questions such as "How can an outer world affect an inner mind," or "How do the acts of mind reach out and lay hold of objects defined in antithesis to them," and, therefore, how "is it possible to know at all" (Dewey 1925a, 19–20). The main question from a transactional point of view is *not* how subject and object can meet each other in the act of knowing, but rather "how and why the whole is distinguished into subject and object, nature and mental operations" (Dewey 1925a, 19).

The idea of transaction denotes, however, not only a method or procedure. It also stands for a more substantive theory, which is partly informed by evolutionary theory and partly by post-Newtonian physics. In this context "transaction" stands for the most general processes in nature. In his earlier writings Dewey described nature as "a moving whole of interacting parts" (1929a, 232). When, in his later writings, he preferred to speak about "transaction," it is because "interaction" still suggests the existence of independent entities that interact ("thing balanced against thing in causal connection"; Dewey and Bentley 1949, 101), while *transaction* puts the process first and treats distinctions such as those between subject and object or between organism and environment as *functional* distinctions emerging from this process—not as starting points or metaphysical givens.

Dewey distinguished the transactional approach from two other approaches. The first is the model of "self-action" in which it is assumed that causes for action are "internal." The second is the model of "inter-action." Dewey credited Galileo for having introduced the latter approach as an alternative to the Aristotelian tradition of self-action. The Newtonian worldview can be seen as the most perfect example of the interactive approach because it conceived of reality as a process of singular forces operating between immutable particles (Dewey and Bentley 1949, 100–106).

While Newtonian physics operated within time and space, the step to the transactional approach was achieved when time and space *themselves* became understood as part of the process. Einstein was most influential in this, of course, although the general idea can already be found in Maxwell's notion of "field" (Dewey and Bentley 1949, 106–9; Dewey 1929a, 102, 115–17). Dewey noticed that with respect to their epistemology, Einstein was actually professing more of a self-actional approach; it was Bohr who took the more consistent transactional view where the process of knowing is no longer conceived as an observation of nature from the outside, but as an intervention into nature and hence as a natural event (Dewey and Bentley 1949, 108–9). This relationship is most famously expressed by the so-called Heisenberg uncertainty principle, in which the very process of observing and measuring subatomic particles has direct consequences on the characteristics of the particles being observed.

Although the methodological and the substantive interpretation of the idea of "transaction" can be distinguished, they are rather closely connected in Dewey's writings:

> Our position is simply that since man as an organism has evolved among other organisms in an evolution called "natural," we are willing under hypothesis to treat all of his behavings, including his most advanced knowings, as activities not of himself alone, nor even as primarily his, but as processes of the full situation of organism-environment. (Dewey and Bentley 1949, 97)

Since Dewey used "*transaction*" to refer to the most general processes in and of nature, his position can be characterized as a kind of *naturalism*. Dewey definitely preferred "*naturalism*" to "*materialism*," not only because he rejects the idea that reality ultimately consists of material particles or entities, but because in a sense the word "*material*" derives its meaning from the distinction between the material and the mental. Since such a distinction obviously has no place in Dewey's philosophy (at least not as an original or ontological distinction), "*naturalism*" seems to be the best—or the least worst—alternative (Dewey and Bentley 1949, 266–67; Dewey 1939b, 86–87).

Dewey's naturalistic transactionalism provides the framework in which he develops his theory of knowledge. In this chapter we discuss the main components of this theory. We start with the central notion of his philosophy, namely, the concept of *experience*. Against this background we then discuss Dewey's philosophy of action. In the third section we focus on Dewey's theory of knowledge. Although in this chapter we do not discuss research directly, all three sections address issues that are of crucial importance for a pragmatist understanding of the research process. Thus, this chapter provides the theoretical background for a pragmatist approach to and understanding of educational research.

EXPERIENCE

"*Experience*" is without doubt the most important concept in Dewey's philosophy, as can be inferred from book titles such as *Experience and Nature* (Dewey 1925a), *Art as Experience* (Dewey 1934b), and *Experience and Education* (Dewey 1938b, 1–62). Experience is, however, also the most problematic notion of his philosophy in that it can easily be misunderstood and misinterpreted—something that Dewey became quite well aware of during his career.

Experience as Transaction

Dewey used the word "*experience*" to refer to the transactions of living organisms and their environment. What is distinctive about these transactions is that this is a *double* relationship (Dewey 1917, 7):

> The organism acts in accordance with its own structure, simple or complex, upon its surroundings. As a consequence the changes produced in the environment react upon the organism and its activities. The living creature undergoes, suffers, the consequences of its own behavior. *This close connection between doing and suffering or undergoing forms what we call experience.* (Dewey 1920, 129; emphasis added)

The last sentence of this quotation provides an important key to Dewey's philosophy. It shows that for Dewey experience is *not*, as is the case in the dualistic tradition of the philosophy of consciousness, "a veil that shuts man [*sic*] off from nature" (Dewey 1925a, 5). This was, for example, what Immanuel Kant suggested when he argued that we can never have any knowledge of the world as it is "in itself" but only of the world as "created" by our senses. It was also the point that David Hume made when he argued that the existence of reality is an interesting and often very useful hypothesis, but nothing more than that because our mind can only be certain of the "data" it receives from the senses, not whether there lies a world "beyond."

What Dewey wanted to stress with his transactional redefinition of experience is that this is the very way in which living organisms are *connected* with reality. Experience, as he put it in his book *Experience and Nature*, "is a means of penetrating continually further into the heart of nature" (1925a, 5).

While experience refers to the transactions of all living organisms and their environments, the difference between the experience "of an oyster or a growing bean vine" (Dewey 1916b, 321) and the experience of human beings is that the latter's experience is always mediated by culture. Human experience is what it is, Dewey wrote, "because human beings are subject to the influences of culture, including use of definite means of intercommunication, and are what in anthropological jargon are called *acculturated* organisms" (1939b, 15). Dewey had an *anthropological* understanding of culture. For him culture is everything that is the product of human action and interaction. The most important cultural product is language, which Dewey defined as everything that has meaning. What is included in this broad definition of language is not only spoken and written language, but also, for example, rituals, ceremonies, monuments, and the products of art and technology. These things and events get their *meaning* from the role they play in coordinated human action, that is, in and by the "conjoint community of functional use" made of them (Dewey 1938a, 52). From this point of view, a style of clothing has meaning because it is used to identify a person as a member of a group (the colors, for instance, of a favorite sports team), or as preparing for a particular activity (a uniform), or as from a particular social background (how formal or expensive it might be).

Modes of Experience

We will return to Dewey's ideas about the way in which meaning emerges out of human cooperation later in the chapter. For now the most important thing to see is that Dewey's definition of experience allows him to restore reality to all dimensions or aspects of the way in which human beings are "in the world." Experience covers the whole range of human possibilities. Dewey referred to these dimensions as *modes* of experience. Knowing is one mode of experience, but it is only one mode among others. Other modes of experience, as we have already seen in the previous chapter, are, for example, the practical mode, the ethical mode, the aesthetic mode, and the religious mode.

The (re)definition of experience as the close connection between the doing and undergoing of living organisms provides Dewey with an answer to the "intellectualistic fallacy," that is the assumption "that all experience is a kind of knowing" (1925a, 28). Dewey's point was that "we do not have to go to knowledge to obtain an exclusive hold on reality," because "the world *as we experience it* is the real world" (1929a, 235, emphasis added).

Dewey's transactional conception of experience clearly solves some of the key problems of the modern, dualistic philosophical tradition. This is not because Dewey provided answers to the questions of this tradition, but because he introduces a new framework and a different set of assumptions. As a result of this maneuver, some of the problems of the modern tradition simply disappear. But this does not mean that there are no questions left for Dewey. One question for Dewey is how the different modes of experience relate to experience more generally. How and under which conditions does experience "move" into, for example, the cognitive or the aesthetic mode? Another question is about the relationship between the different modes of experience. What, for example, is the relationship between the ethical and the cognitive modes? For our discussion of educational research, the most important mode is the cognitive mode of experience, although it is clearly related to the others. The cognitive mode also occupies a central place in Dewey's writings. It is only relatively late in his career that he started to write more extensively about the other modes of experience (1934a, 1–58; 1934b; 1939a, 189–252).

Although Dewey rejected the idea that knowledge is the measure of reality, this rejection does not imply a derogation of the importance of knowledge. Dewey characterized knowing as the mode of experience that supports action. Knowing has to do with the relationship between our actions and their consequences. It is because of this that knowledge can help us to get a better control over our actions, at least better than in the case of blind trial and error. "Where there is the possibility of control," Dewey wrote, "knowledge is the sole agency of its realization" (1925a, 29). "*Control*" here does not mean complete mastery, but the ability to intelligently plan and direct our actions and their likely consequences. This ability is first of all important in those situations in which we are not sure how to act—which is expressed in one of Dewey's descriptions of knowing as having to do with "the transformation of disturbed and unsettled situations into those more controlled and more significant" (1929a, 236). Knowing is also important, however, in order to achieve more control, a more intelligent approach in the other domains of experience; knowing "facilitates control of objects for purposes of non-cognitive experience" (Dewey 1929a, 79).

Notwithstanding the importance of knowledge, Dewey argues neither that control is the only way in which human beings should relate to their natural and social environment, nor that the value of the other modes of experience *depends* on the cognitive mode. The following statement makes quite clear where Dewey stood on this:

Not all existence asks to be known, and certainly does not ask leave from thought to exist. But some existences as they are experienced do ask thought to direct them in their course so that they may be ordered and fair and be such as to commend themselves to admiration, approval and appreciation. Knowledge affords the sole means by which this direction can be effected. (1929a, 236)

The background for Dewey's discussion of the cognitive mode of experience is to be found in his theory of action, to which we will turn next. We go into some detail about Dewey's psychological views and theory of learning, not only because in a book on educational research these may be of interest to the reader, but more because they form the foundation for Dewey's understanding of knowledge and the way in which knowledge is acquired. In this respect Dewey's psychology of action provides the framework for his understanding of inquiry and research.

ACTION

Dewey articulated the framework of his theory of action in an article called "The Reflex Arc Concept in Psychology," which was published in 1896 (EW5: 96–109). This article has become a classic in the history of modern psychology and is commonly identified as the beginning of the functionalist approach in psychology (Titchener 1898; Langfeld 1943; Leahey 1987). The key idea of psychological functionalism is that it does not conceive of psychological phenomena such as "*perception*," "*consciousness*," or "*mind*" as entities on their own, but accounts for these phenomena by making clear how they emerge from more general processes to perform a specific *function*. Dewey credited Darwin for having made this change of perspective from "essence" to "function" possible (1909b, 7–8).

Dewey's Critique and Reconstruction of the Reflex Arc Model

Dewey developed his functionalism in the context of a critique of dualistic thought in psychology. Interestingly enough, he did not focus his critique on old psychological theories, but rather addressed something that was relatively new in his time, namely, the use in psychological theory of the biological structure of the "reflex arc," that is, the system of

afferent nerves, central nervous system, and efferent nerves. This structure had already been used successfully for the explanation of elementary
patterns of movement in lower animals. By the end of the nineteenth century psychologists were starting to use it to explain human behavior in
terms of sensory stimulus, central processing, and motor response—a development that would eventually lead to the stimulus-response psychology of behaviorism.

Dewey's main point of critique against this view was not that biology
was used to understand human action, but that the principles of explanation and classification that the reflex arc idea wanted to replace were not
sufficiently replaced. The "new psychology" was still dualistic. Dewey argued that the older dualism between sensation and idea "is repeated in the
current dualism of peripheral and central structures and functions," while
the older dualism of body and soul "finds a distinct echo in the current dualism of stimulus and response" (1896, 96). The only way to overcome
these dualistic views is by *not* starting from disjointed parts (stimulus,
processing, response) and then to ask how these parts hang together, but
to begin with the process "all the way around" (Coughlan 1975, 129). In
Dewey's case this process is the organism-environment transaction.

One of the problems with the stimulus-response theory is that it assumes that it is the stimulus that sets the organism in motion. Dewey argued, however, that the organism, as long as it is alive, is *always already*
in motion. This not only means that what comes before a stimulus "is a
whole act, a sensory-motor coordination" (1896, 100), it also means that
the stimulus can only be "a *change* in the environment connected with a
change in activity," just as a response is not simply a behavior "but marks
a *change* in behavior" (Dewey 1930a, 224). When we are driving a car
and someone crosses the street unexpectedly, we could say that the person
crossing is the stimulus and our pressing the brake the response to this
stimulus. What Dewey wants to emphasize, however, is that we shouldn't
understand our response as a way of coming into action. We are already
active—we are driving the car—and we adjust to the change in the situation by a change in our action.

While the terms are similar, this dynamic model yields quite a different
psychological model than behaviorism. Dewey characterized the organism-
environment transaction as a process of continuous readjustment, not simply as an external stimulus and then an organism's response. Through se-
lection and assimilation the organism establishes a dynamic coordination
with its environment. The increase of the *range* of coordination is one of

the central developmental processes. Distinct functions, such as the ability to use the eyes "as motor organs in order to control the stimulus of light" can be seen as the outcome of the coordination of several minor coordinations (Dewey 1899, 181). Once this coordination—which in ordinary language is called "seeing"—has reached a certain level of agility, the coordination of this function with other functions becomes possible (for example, in eye-hand coordination). Dewey argued that the coordination of such functions is a crucial step forward, in that it involves "the dawning of intelligence hardly describable" (1899, 184).

Dewey connected coordination with the dawning of intelligence because increased coordination implies a change and increase of *meaning*. When there is a translation from the terms of one activity into another, for example, from seeing something to reaching and handling it, then the meaning of what is seen changes, because what is seen is now (also) seen *as* something that can be reached and handled. According to Dewey it is this "cross-reference, this mutuality of excitation and direction, which constitutes the essence of intelligence wherever found" (1899, 184).

A Transactional Definition of Stimulus and Response

The central point of Dewey's critique of the reflex arc model, then, lies in his recognition of the fact that a stimulus cannot be something that comes from the "outside" to set the organism into motion (which also implies that a response cannot be understood as the motion that is caused by the stimulus). The organism is always already active; the organism is always already maintaining a dynamic balance with its environment. This does not mean, however, that we can no longer use the concepts of "*stimulus*" and "*response*," but if we want to use them, Dewey argued, we need to see them as "divisions of labor, functioning factors, within the single concrete whole, now designated the reflex arc" (1896, 97) and not as "distinctions of existence" (1896, 104). In redefining stimulus and response, Dewey distinguished between two different situations: one in which the connection between stimulus and response has already been established, and one in which this is not (yet) the case. The latter situation is especially important, because it provides the action-theoretical framework for Dewey's theory of knowledge and for his understanding of inquiry and research.

Dewey referred to the first situation as one of "accomplished adaptation," such as in the case of instincts or well-formed habits. If in such a situation we use the terms "*stimulus*" and "*response*," these terms do not refer to sensation and motion. They rather refer to complete *acts,* which, in an ordered sequence, contribute to the achievement of a specific end. In such a situation we have "a continuously ordered sequence of *acts*, all adapted in themselves and in the order of their sequences, to reach a certain objective end" (Dewey 1896, 104). If in this context we refer to one act as a stimulus and to another as a response, we mean no more than that seen from the point of view of a specific end, we have an ordered sequence of acts working together to achieve this end. This means that "*stimulus*" and "*response*" can only be used retrospectively, because we can only identify the connection within the sequence and the contribution of each of the steps in achieving the end, once we know how the individual acts have contributed to achieving this end. For example, one can say that a red light (stimulus) *caused* someone to press on their brake (response) only when one understands the complex rules of traffic laws and driving a car—otherwise one can only say that one event *followed* the other, not necessarily because of it. Since the distinction between stimulus and response relies on the existence of an end (in Greek: *telos*) this distinction is *teleological*.

The situation is quite different when a coordination has not yet been established. In such a situation the organism does not "know" how to respond. Or to put it in terms of action: There is not one act or pattern of action that immediately presents itself as appropriate. In this case we could say that a *response* is lacking; but we could also say that the *stimulus* is not (yet) clear. These are simply two sides of the same coin: "The real problem may equally well be stated as either to discover the right stimulus, to constitute the stimulus, or to discover, to constitute, the response" (Dewey 1896, 106). According to Dewey it is at this juncture that the distinction of stimulus as sensation and response as motion arises. But the stimulus is *not* a passive sensation, nor is the response something that follows automatically from it. Something isn't a stimulus *until* there is a recognition of and response to it; the two are mutually constituting. The organism actively has to search for the stimulus. The organism has to search, in other words, "for the state of things which decides how a beginning coordination should be completed" (Dewey 1896, 107). And it is "the motor response or attention which constitutes that, which finally becomes the stimulus to another act" (Dewey 1896, 101–2). When we want to cross a street, for example, it is not that we first look at the situation, then close our eyes and cross. We are constantly "scanning" the environment, by the movement of our eyes, our head, and our body; even when we start crossing we keep doing so. It may be that at some point we sense something that interrupts our activity. We then need to focus our attention—Do I hear a car coming from around the corner?—in adjusting our actions accordingly.

Dewey referred to this search for the stimulus as "perception." It is important to see that perception is not something that *precedes* action but has to be conceived as a "factor in organic action" (Dewey 1912, 8). After all, the organism cannot stop its activities to find out what the stimulus actually is. The only way in which the organism can find out the conditions of further action is by tentatively trying out different lines of action. Initially the activities of the organism are uncoordinated and indefinite. But an indefinite (re)action "may have a certain focusing that will further define its subject-matter so that it will afford the stimulus to a more effective subsequent response, and so on" (Dewey 1912, 23–24). While this process can be characterized as that of finding or constituting the stimulus, it is important to keep in mind that the stimulus is only found at the very moment in which the (adequate) response has been found. It is only when the organism has "hit" upon an adequate response, that coordination is achieved, that the organism "knows" what the stimulus was.

Since it is here that we find the very foundation of Dewey's understanding of knowledge, it is worthwhile to quote him at some length about how we should precisely understand this process of the constitution or "construction" of the stimulus through experimental action:

> External movements are involved in the activities of the organism. If and in so far as these activities are indeterminate, there is neither a total, or adequate stimulus . . . nor an adequate total response by the organism. Adequate stimulus and adequate response are both delayed. . . . The partial responses, however, are neither merely dispersed miscellaneously upon the environment, nor are they merely possible. They are directed upon the partial stimuli so as to *convert* them into a single coordinated stimulus. Then a total response of the organism follows. This functional transformation of the environment under conditions of uncertain action into conditions for determining an appropriate organic response constitutes perception. (1912, 19)

Habits and Meaning

The *act* of perception—which is not the same as sensation—results, if successful, in coordinated action. More generally we can say that an earlier "open" phase in which there is a tension of various elements of organic energy, resolves into a later "closed" phase of integrated interaction of organism and environment. Dewey stressed that in the case of higher organisms the outcome of this process on the side of the organism is not identical with the state out of which disequilibration and tension emerged. There rather is "a change in the organic structures that conditions further behavior" (1938a, 38). The behavior of the organism becomes more specific or more focused. This modification is what Dewey called a *habit*. Habits, which are "the basis of organic learning" (Dewey 1938a, 38), are not, or are only in specific cases, patterns of action but should be understood as *predispositions* to act: "The essence of habits is an acquired predisposition to *ways* or modes of response, not to particular acts. . . . Habit means special sensitiveness or accessibility to certain classes of stimuli, standing predilections and aversions, rather than bare recurrence of specific acts" (Dewey 1922b, 32).

Three things are important in Dewey's notion of habit. The first is that habits are *not* formed by sheer repetition. The reason for this is simple, since the ability to repeat can only be the *result* of the formation of a habit. This is not to deny that repetition is possible. But since action always involves the organism-environment transaction, repetition is only likely to occur as far as environing conditions remain the same. Dewey stressed that sheer repetition in the case of human organisms "is the product of conditions that are uniform because they have been made so mechanically" (1938a, 39). But such habits are limited in their manifestation and certainly do not provide the model upon which Dewey's theory of habit formation and operation is framed.

Second, since action is always transaction, it follows that the same environmental conditions will not necessarily evoke the same "response" in different organisms. All depends upon prior learning, that is, the unique set of habits that each individual organism acquires over time.

Third—and this insight is crucial for an accurate understanding of Dewey's position—habits can be seen as the organic basis of meaning. To understand the link between habits and meaning it is first of all important to see that Dewey does not think of meaning as something mental. For Dewey meaning is primarily "a property of behavior" (1925a, 141). It is the way in which the organism responds to the environment. As long as a coordination has not been established, that is, as long as the organism has not found a response that will result in coordination, we can therefore say that the *meaning* of the situation is not clear. Finding a response that brings about coordination is therefore the same as saying that the meaning of the situation for *this* organism has become clear.

The link between *habit* and *meaning* is not one in which one word is simply replaced by another. Dewey's point is that the experimental transaction of organism-environment not only leads to more specific habits, but also results in a more "differentiated," more meaningful world. Our responses become more specific, and as a result the world to which we respond becomes more differentiated. This is what Dewey had in mind when he wrote that habit means "special sensitiveness or accessibility to certain classes of stimuli" (1922b, 32). The world is no longer "a vast penumbra of vague, unfigured things" but gradually becomes "a figured framework of objects" (Dewey 1922b, 128). What should not be forgotten is that these objects have a strictly transactional status; objects are "events with meaning" (Dewey 1925a, 240).

An example of these ideas can be found in the case of someone who starts to play the piano. Initially it will be quite difficult to find the C key on the piano, even more so in response to seeing a black dot on a sheet of music. But as a result of experimentation, that is, of practicing and trying things out, the beginning pianist acquires more specific predispositions, more specific habits. Eventually our pianist will not only be able to immediately touch the right keys upon seeing the notes on a sheet of music; the piano will also start to appear differently to our pianist who will, upon looking at the keyboard, no longer see an indiscriminable and confusing collection of keys, but will immediately see where the C key is, where octaves are, and so on. This is how the world becomes meaningful, that is, how objects emerge from the field of transaction.

A Theory of Experimental Learning

One way to summarize Dewey's theory of action is to say that it amounts to *a theory of experimental learning*. Dewey characterized living organisms—including the human organism—as capable of establishing and maintaining a dynamic, coordinated transaction with its environment. Through this process the predispositions of the organism become more focused and specific, which is another way of saying that through the tentative, experimental way of establishing coordinated transaction, the organism has *learned*. This learning is, however, not the acquisition of information about how the world "out there" really is. It is learning in the sense of the acquisition of a complex set of predispositions to act. In this process the world becomes more differentiated. It becomes, in other words, infused with meaning. This theory of learning also lies at the basis of Dewey's understanding of inquiry and research. Dewey suggests, so we could say, that we understand inquiry and research as processes of experiential and experimental learning, which result in more diverse ways of action, reflection, and understanding. We will return to this in chapter 3.

From Action to Intelligent Action

As we have seen, the notion of "habit" occupies a central position in Dewey's theory of action. Dewey argued that human beings are creatures of habit, "not of reason nor yet of instinct" (1922b, 88). Dewey even argued that there is no "ready-made self" behind our habits. Habits should therefore not be understood as tools that can be picked up and used at will. The use itself *is* the habit, and "we are the habit" (Dewey 1922b, 21). Since habits are not part of our endowment at birth but are "acquired predispositions," the transaction with the environment—natural and social— is crucial in the transformation of "impulses" into habits. Dewey preferred to use the word "*impulse*" instead of "*instinct*," because the latter word is "still too laden with the older notion that an instinct is always definitely organized and adapted—which for the most part is just what it is not in human beings" (Dewey 1922b, 75).

Some would argue that if the development of habits depends on transactions with the environment, that this would imply a restriction of human freedom. This is, however, not how Dewey saw it: "To view institutions as enemies of freedom, and all conventions as slavery, is to deny the only means by which positive freedom in action can be secured. . . . Convention and custom are necessary to carrying forward impulse to any happy conclusion" (1922b, 155). The problem lies not with convention as such, but with "stupid and rigid convention" (Dewey 1922b, 115). This suggests that it is possible to go beyond mere habitual convention. We touch upon the most crucial aspect of Dewey's theory of action for our purposes here, namely the assumption that it is possible to transform habits into *intelligent* habits, and action into *intelligent* action. At one level, we might say this is the purpose of all inquiry and research, including educational research.

The transition from habits to intelligent habits is made possible by the intervention of *thinking*. Thinking is not an original "capacity" of the human organism, but itself something that is acquired. Dewey acknowledged that there must be a distinctive impulse to think, but only in the sense "in which there is an impulse to aviate, to run a typewriter or write stories for magazines" (1922b, 130). Thinking is, in other words, one human possibility among an almost infinite number of other possibilities. All depends on the conditions and cultivations. Dewey's comments about the origin of "knowledge-getting" paint a very clear picture of his position:

> Having hit upon knowledge accidentally, as it were, and the product being liked and its importance noted, knowledge-getting becomes, upon occasion, a definite occupation. And education confirms the disposition, as it may confirm that of a musician or carpenter or tennis-player. But there is no more an original separate impulse or power in one case than in the other. (1922b, 130)

In terms of "impulse" and "habit," the first step in Dewey's account of the emergence of thinking is not different from what we have already seen in terms of "stimulus" and "response." The organism-environment transaction becomes disrupted when an impulse is activated in the organism, which tends to initiate several different and incompatible lines of action, several different, incompatible and conflicting habits. The way out of this situation is basically achieved through "a redistribution of the elements of organized activity between those that have been respectively central and subsidiary," which "concludes in a coming to terms of the old habit and the new impulse" (Dewey 1922b, 125).

In this process, thinking does not yet play a role. The reconstruction and reconstitution of coordination results from the experimental, tentative cooperation of habit, impulse, and perception. The quality of this process does alter, however, when different possible lines of action are systematically explored. This is what Dewey referred to as *deliberation*: "an experiment of finding out what the various lines of possible action are really like. It is an experiment in making various combinations of selected elements of habits and impulses, to see what the resulting action would be like if it were entered upon" (1922b, 132–33). The main problem with such an experiment is, of course, that it is irreversible. The way to address this problem is to experiment with different lines of action in imagination instead of through overt action. This is precisely what thinking does. It is the "dramatic rehearsal (in imagination) of various competing possible lines of action" (Dewey 1922b, 132).

Dewey argued that thinking has an organic basis. Deliberation means that activity is disintegrated, and that its various elements hold one another up. While none has force enough to become the center of a redirected activity, or to dominate a course of action, each has enough power to check others from exercising mastery. In such a situation, Dewey argued, "activity does not cease in order to give way to reflection; activity is turned from execution into intra-organic channels, resulting in dramatic rehearsal" (1922b, 133). The choice for one specific line of action should be understood as "hitting in imagination upon an object which furnishes an adequate stimulus to the recovery of overt action" (Dewey 1922b, 134). Whether this choice will actually lead to coordinated action will, of course, only become clear when the organism actually acts. Deliberation can in no way guarantee that the response will be successful. But what it can do is make the process of choosing more reasonable, more intelligent than would be the case with "blind" trial and error.

Dewey stressed that deliberation cannot be based on the actual consequences of different lines of actions, since these consequences can neither be known nor predicted. The issue is not to ascertain which lines of action are most desirable, but which lines of action are *possible*: "The object of foresight of consequences is not to predict the future. It is to ascertain the meaning of present activities and to secure, so far as possible, a present activity with a unified meaning" (Dewey 1922b, 134). In our example of crossing a street, this means that when we try to identify a sound we hear, the point is not to establish what this sound will bring; it first and foremost is to identify it as possibly being a car coming from around the corner, so that we can adjust our actions to this meaning of the sound.

Symbols and Symbolic Action

While the foregoing makes clear how thinking as dramatic rehearsal intervenes in the process of the constitution of the stimulus to make the deliberation more "intelligent," it does not yet make clear how this dramatic rehearsal itself is possible. Dewey's answer to this question brings us to the third and final component of his account of intelligent action.

The answer to this last question is, as such, not difficult. Dramatic rehearsal relies on the use of *symbols*: "By means of symbols . . . we act without acting. That is, we perform experiments by means of symbols which have results which are themselves only symbolized, and which do not therefore commit us to actual or existential consequences" (Dewey 1929a, 121). The real question is, of course, how we should conceive of this "capacity" to use symbols. Again, Dewey's answer is naturalistic and functionalistic. The naturalistic part of Dewey's answer is that the ability to use symbols is not innate, but a human possibility that must have been hit upon "accidentally, as a by-product, and then employed intentionally" (Dewey 1929a, 121). This is in no way to derogate the importance of symbols. On the contrary, the "discovery" of symbols and symbolization is doubtless "by far the single greatest event in the history of man" (Dewey 1929a, 121) since this affords "the only way of escape from submergence in existence" (Dewey 1929a, 129).

The functionalistic part of Dewey's answer was based on his ideas about human communication. Since Dewey took his point of departure in action and not in consciousness, his conception of communication is *not* one of the transmission of information from one mind to another mind. Dewey instead conceived of communication as a process of the mutual coordination of action. Communication is "the establishment of cooperation in an activity in which there are partners, and in which the activity of each is modified and regulated by partnership" (1925a, 66). This is *not* a process in which *A* simply reacts to *B*'s movements, after which *B* reacts to *A*'s reaction, and so on. Dewey's point was that successful coordination requires that *A* reacts to what *B* *intends* to achieve with his activities, just as *B* reacts to what *A* intends to achieve with his activities. Successful coordination requires that the partners in interaction each try to *anticipate* the other's actions. To understand, Dewey wrote, "is to anticipate together, it is to make a cross-reference which, when acted upon, brings about a partaking in a common, inclusive, undertaking" (1925a, 141). Successful coordination requires, in other words, that the partners in interaction react to the *meaning* of each other's actions, which means that they take each other's actions as *symbols* for what is not (yet) there.

Dewey stressed that this is not a process in which one actor simply has to adapt himself to the meaning of the activities of the other actor. It is a much more complex process in which there is constant mutual anticipatory adjustment. This becomes clear in the following example, in which *A* asks *B* to bring him a flower:

> *B* upon hearing *A*, makes a preparatory reaction of his eyes, hands and legs in view of the consummatory act of *A*'s possession; he engages in the act of grasping, carrying and tendering the flower to *A*. At the same time, *A* makes a preparatory response to *B*'s consummatory act, that of carrying and proffering the flower. Thus neither the sound uttered by *A*, his gesture of pointing, nor the sight of the thing pointed to, is the occasion and stimulus of *B*'s act; the stimulus is *B*'s anticipatory share in the consummation of a transaction in which both partake. (Dewey 1925a, 179)

The point here is that successful cooperation requires the partners in interaction "to see and inquire from a standpoint that is not strictly personal but is common to them as participants or "parties" in a conjoint undertaking" (Dewey 1938a, 52). This standpoint does not exist initially within the partners in interaction, nor is it something objective. It rather is created through the process of communication. In this sense communication is a thoroughly creative process: "Something is literally made in common in at least two different centers of behavior" (Dewey 1925a, 141).

When Dewey claimed that symbols are the product of social interaction, this is first of all in the sense in which the success of cooperation depends on the ability to anticipate, that is, to take the activities of the partner in interaction as symbols standing for what the other wants to achieve. Further, it is because the "*things*"—in the widest sense of this word—that make shared action possible, acquire significance, become things-with-meaning (that is, symbols), as a result of this very process:

> In the first place, it is the *motion and sounds* of A which have meaning, or are signs. Similarly the movements of B, while they are immediate to him, are signs to A of B's cooperation or refusal. But secondarily the *thing* pointed out by A to B gains meaning. It ceases to be just what it brutely is at the moment, and is responded to in its potentiality, as a means to remoter consequences. (Dewey 1925a, 142)

This is not only the case with such things as flowers. It is also the way in which a sound or a written mark becomes a word, in that it gains meaning "when its use establishes a genuine community of action" (Dewey 1925a, 145). Meaning is therefore a "method of action," it is "a way of using things as means to a shared consummation" (Dewey 1925a, 147). It is against this background that Dewey made the comparison between language and tools, because "a tool is a thing used as a means to consequences, instead of being taken directly and physically" (1925a, 146).

KNOWLEDGE

The foregoing discussion of Dewey's understanding of experience and action provides us with all the main elements of Dewey's theory of knowledge. Dewey's view of knowledge is about reflection and action, and about the reflective transformation of experience understood as transactional. Our account of Dewey's theory of knowledge in this section is intended to elaborate his theory of knowledge in less psychological and more philosophical terms, since the latter is the vocabulary of research.

The Reality of Experience

We have seen that Dewey's transactional (re)definition of experience makes it possible to restore the reality of *all* dimensions of experience. Dewey put an end to the idea that it is only through knowledge that we can obtain a hold on reality. All modes of experience are equally real since they are all modes of the transaction of living organisms and their environments. Yet Dewey argued that experience is also real in another sense—and the latter point is of crucial importance for an adequate understanding of the difference between experience and cognitive experience, "a distinction without which my view cannot be understood" (Dewey 1939b, 33).

In an article from 1905 called "The Postulate of Immediate Empiricism," Dewey claimed that "things—anything, everything, in the ordinary or non-technical use of the term "thing"—*are what they are experienced as*" (158, emphasis added). This first of all means that everyone's experience is equally real. The horse trader, the jockey, the zoologist, and the paleontologist will all have their own experience of a horse. If their accounts turn out to be different, there is, however, no reason for assuming that the content of only one of them can be real and that the experiences of the others must necessarily be any less accurate or real. It simply reflects the fact that a horse trader will have a different experience of the horse than a zoologist does because the trader "enters" the transaction from a different standpoint, from a different background, from a different history, and with different purposes and intentions. We don't have a contrast, therefore, between reality and various approximations to it; what we have are "different reals of experience" (Dewey 1905, 159).

Dewey's postulate further implies that what is experienced is itself real. If someone is flustered by a noise, then that noise *is* fearsome. Dewey stressed that "it *really* is, not merely phenomenally or subjectively so" (Dewey 1905, 160). This claim must, of course, be understood transactionally; if someone is frightened by a sound, then the fear is the immediate response of the organism. The sound *is* frightening because the organism reacts to the sound as being a frightening-sound. This implies, however, that *being* frightened is not the same as knowing that one *is* frightened. Knowing what *caused* the fearsome noise (for example, a burglar or a blow of wind) is a different experience. While this experience might be more *true* than the original experience of "being afraid," it is definitely not more *real* than that experience: "The question of truth is not as to whether Being or Non-Being, Reality or mere Appearance is experienced, but as to the *worth* of a certain concretely experienced thing" (Dewey 1905, 163).

This is also the case for those experiences that are clearly illusory. Dewey discussed the optical illusion of Zöllner's lines, which are lines that are experienced as convergent but in fact are parallel. If things are what they are experienced to be, how then can we make the distinction between illusion and the true state of affairs? The answer to this question is *not* to be found in the experience as such. When we experience the lines as divergent, then "the lines of *that* experience *are* divergent; not merely *seem* so" (Dewey 1905, 163). If there is a difference, it has to do with the *value or meaning of this experience*: "[A]s manifestations of interactions of a naturally existent organism and existent environing conditions all experienced materials stand on exactly the same level. But it does *not* mean that with respect to their *evidential* value, their function as dependable signs, they stand on the same level" (Dewey 1939b, 26). This not only means that experience is always real, so that we do not have to go to knowledge to establish its reality. It also means that experience as such— and the "as such" is, as we will see, very important here—does not give us any knowledge. Dewey rejected, in other words, the idea that experience provides us with elementary "bits" of cognition, which, when put together in a systematic or logical manner, result in knowledge (which is the view of "logical positivism," the position developed by members of the *Vienna Circle*; see chapter 1).

From Experience to Knowledge

The difference between experience and knowledge is therefore to be found in the *happening* of experience. The office of knowledge, Dewey wrote, is "to discover the conditions and consequences" of its happening (1929a, 84). It signifies a search "for those relations upon which the *occurrence* of real qualities and values depends" (Dewey 1929a, 83). In this respect, knowledge is intimately and necessarily connected with action, because the discovery of the conditions and consequences of experience "can take place only by modifying the given qualities in such ways that *relations* become manifest" (Dewey 1929a, 84).

The shift from understanding knowledge as being concerned with the world "as it is" to understanding knowledge as being concerned with *conditions and consequences*, is a very important element of Dewey's theory of knowledge—an element with crucial implications for our understanding of research (see chapter 5). It represents a shift from a concern with things as they are to a concern with "the history to which a given thing belongs" (Dewey 1925a, 243). It is, to put it differently, a shift from "knowing as an aesthetic enjoyment of the properties of nature as a world of divine art, to knowing as a means of secular control—this is, a method of purposefully introducing changes which will alter the direction of the course of events" (Dewey 1929a, 81).

This shift also implies that knowledge is concerned with relations and not with reality "as such." The most prominent relation is that between (our) actions and (their) consequences. Along these lines action introduces the dimension of *time* into the heart of our understanding of knowledge. For this reason we can say that Dewey had a *temporal conception of knowledge*. The first step in this temporal theory is concerned with the question of how experience becomes cognitive experience, how, in other words, experience turns into the cognitive "mode."

The Temporal Development of Experience

Dewey assumed that different modes of experience do not occur simultaneously but alternate. This means that it is only at a certain moment and for specific purposes that experience turns into the cognitive mode and that, when the work is done, experience returns to another, noncognitive mode. From this point of view the question of knowledge is no longer the epistemological question about the relationship of "thought as such to reality as such" (Dewey 1903b, 302). It now is an empirical question about what it is that makes us alternately live in a world of experience in which knowledge plays no role and a world of experience, which is thoroughly concerned with knowledge.

Dewey's answer to this question brings us back to familiar terrain, since he argued that knowledge arises

> because of the appearance of incompatible factors within the empirical situation. . . . Then opposed responses are provoked which cannot be taken simultaneously in overt action, and which accordingly can be dealt with, whether simultaneously or successively, only after they have been brought into a plan of organized action. (Dewey 1916b, 326)

The problem is one of the *meaning* of the situation—and for Dewey "situation" includes both organism and environment. Since for Dewey meaning is a property of behavior, we can describe the aforementioned situation as one that, through calling out opposed modes of behavior, presents itself as *meaning* incompatible things (1916b, 326–27). The only way to solve the problem—that is the only way to solve it in an *intelligent* manner and not by simple trial and error—is by means of a systematic inspection of the situation. On the one hand, we need to identify and state the problem. On the other hand, we need to develop suggestions for solving the problem, for finding a way to act—*and hence to find out what the meaning of the situation actually is*.

While thought or reflection must play an important part in this process, it will not result in knowledge. Thinking *as thinking*, Dewey stressed, "gets no farther . . . than a statement of elements constituting the difficulty at hand and a statement . . . of a method for resolving them" (1916b, 327). It is only when action follows, that is, when we *use* the suggested solution to guide our action, that the value of both the analysis of the problem and the suggested solution can be established. We need overt action to determine the worth and validity of our reflective considerations. Otherwise we have, at most, a hypothesis about the problem and a hypothesis about its possible solution.

This means that in order to get knowledge we need action. But although action is a necessary condition for knowledge, it is not a sufficient one. We also need thinking or reflection. Dewey's claim was that it is the *combination* of reflection and action that leads to knowledge: "[E]xperience as an interaction consists of connections between doing-undergoing-doing . . . , and the connections between the two, *when they are noted and formulated*, give rise to the distinctively cognitive experience" (1939b, 17). Or with a more vivid example:

> To run against a hard and painful stone is not in itself . . . an act of knowing; but if running into a hard and painful thing is an outcome predicted after inspection of data and elaboration of a hypothesis, then the hardness and the painful bruise which define the thing as stone also constitute it emphatically as an object of knowledge. (1916b, 329)

From this it also follows that knowing—the acquisition of knowledge—is not something that takes place somewhere deep down inside the human mind. Knowing is itself an activity, it is "literally something which we do" (Dewey 1916b, 367): "Knowing consists of operations that give experienced objects a form in which the relations, upon which the onward course of events depends, are securely experienced" (Dewey 1929a, 235).

The Meaning of Knowledge

This in turn implies that the meaning that results from the reflective transformation of an "indeterminate" situation into a determinate situation (coordinated transaction) is of a specific nature. Dewey wrote that the meaning that emerges from the restoration of coordinated action is a meaning or experience "which is contemporaneously aware of meaning something beyond itself" (Dewey 1906b, 113). This "beyond" is not simply present or will not simply become present in the future. It will only become present "through the intervention of an operation" (Dewey 1906b, 113–14), that is, through what we do. When experience is "cognitional," it means that we perceive something as meaning-something-else-that-we-will-experience-when-we-act-in-a-specific-way. A very precise description of this idea can be found in the following passage:

> An experience is a knowledge, if in its quale there is an experienced distinction and connection between two elements of the following sort: *one means or intends the presence of the other in the same fashion in which it itself is already present, while the other is that which, while not present in the same fashion, must become so present if the meaning or intention of its companion or yoke-fellow is to be fulfilled through the operation it sets up.* (Dewey 1906b, 114–15, emphasis in original)

It is precisely along these lines that knowledge is related to the possibility of control: "In knowledge," Dewey wrote, "causes become means and effects become consequences, and thereby things having meaning" (1929a, 236). Knowledge has, in other words, to do with *inference*. Dewey defined inference as a reaction to something that in time or place is distant: "The instigation to behave toward the remote in space or time is the primary trait of the inferential act; descriptively speaking, the act consists in taking up an attitude of response to an absent thing as if it were present" (1915b, 70).

Because inference is a step into an unknown future, it is a precarious journey. Inference, that is, behaving in the given situation on the basis of something that is not yet given, always involves uncertainty and risk. A stone, Dewey argued, can only react to stimuli of the present, not of the future, and for that reason cannot make mistakes. Since inference entails the possibility of mistake, it introduces truth and falsity into the world (Dewey 1915b, 70).

One further thing that should be noted here is that the inferential response is, as such, as immediate as the "original" response. Once the meaning of a thing has been established as meaning something else, the organism will simply respond to the thing-as-meaning-something-else. The meaning of the thing has simply changed. There is no distinction between the thing and what it means: "There are no alternatives save either acceptance or rejection *in toto*" (Dewey 1915b, 75). This implies that what is needed for control is some device by which the inferences can be treated for what they are, namely, *inferred* things, that is *possibilities* or *meanings*. What is needed is a way to consider "fire" as one of the possible meanings of "smoke." In order for this to become possible, we need to create "new objects." We must take something ("any kind of physical existence"; Dewey 1916b, 351) to stand for fire-in-its-status-as-inferred. This thing is "a meaning" or a symbol, and as we have already seen, it is only when we have symbols that deliberation, reflection, and intelligent action can become possible.

Events and Objects

In our discussion of Dewey's theory of action we have already seen that the experimental transaction of organism-environment leads both to more specific habits and to a more "differentiated" world. Our responses, our patterns of action, become more specific, and as a result, the world to which we respond becomes more differentiated, as well. The world gradually becomes "a figured framework of objects" (Dewey 1922b, 128). This is the context for Dewey's claim that we should think of objects as "events with meaning" (Dewey 1925a, 240). The objects of our experience, the objects that we immediately see around us, are therefore not the *starting-point* of the acquisition of knowledge, but its *outcome*. This implies that the process of acquiring knowledge should not be understood as a process in which we are trying to get knowledge about the objects in the world. Those objects are already constituted by our knowledge—not necessarily knowledge that we are aware of, but definitely the "knowledge" that lives "in the muscles," the knowledge that lives in our habits.

Dewey suggested that the acquiring of meaning by sounds, in virtue of which they become words, is perhaps "the most striking illustration that can be found of the way in which mere sensory stimuli acquire definiteness and constancy of meaning and are thereby themselves defined and interconnected for purposes of recognition" (Dewey 1933, 231): "Language is a good example because there are hundreds or even thousands of words in which meaning is now so thoroughly consolidated with physical qualities as to be directly understood" (Dewey 1933, 231). Words, to put it differently, are events that have acquired meaning. Words are "sound-events" that, through a process of experimental learning, have become "objects"—events with meaning.

In the case of language it is relatively easy to see that words, or word-sounds, don't have a meaning of their own, but that they have *become* meaningful entities over time. It is far more difficult to draw the same conclusion with respect to physical objects, such as chairs, tables, trees, stones, hills, and flowers, "where it seems as if the union of intellectual meaning with physical fact were aboriginal" (Dewey 1933, 231). Yet chairs and tables are as much events with meaning—meaningful transactions—as words are. And their meaning is strictly transactional, that is, it is the outcome of the specific ways in which a successful relationship between the antecedents and consequences of experience was established.

It is for precisely this reason that Dewey argued that we should think of objects as tools: "The character of an object is like that of a tool . . . ; it is an order of determination of sequential changes terminating in a foreseen consequence" (1925a, 121). With this transactional understanding of objects, Dewey implicitly rejected the idea that our knowledge is "of" or "about" the objects in the world. It is not that through a process of inquiry we can find out what the possible meanings of a chair are. Rather, a chair specifies a particular way in which the transaction with the environment has become meaningful.

Dewey's own example was about the "existence" to which we commonly refer to as "paper." There are many different ways to transact (successfully) with this "existence":

> It signifies something to start a fire with; something like snow; made of wood-pulp; manufactured for profit; property in the legal sense; a definite combination illustrative of certain principles of chemical science; an article the invention of which has made a tremendous difference in human history, and so on indefinitely. (Dewey 1925a, 241)

Does this list signify a range of possible meanings of the thing called "paper"? Dewey argued that we should instead say that we have a situation where the same "existential events" (Dewey 1925a, 241) are capable of an infinite number of meanings. If we would say that it is "paper" that has all these different meanings, we are only saying that *the word "paper"* is the most used or the preferred meaning of the existential events capable of entering into all these different transactions. But there is no way in which we can claim that the word *"paper"* is the most original, most fundamental, or first meaning of this event. All we are saying is that "its existence is not exhausted in its being paper, although paper is its ordinary meaning for human intercourse" (Dewey 1925a, 241).

Truth and Correspondence

The final element of Dewey's temporal theory of knowledge that concerns us here has to do with the question of (the) truth (of our knowledge). We have already seen that for Dewey there is no sense in asking about the truth of our immediate experience. Immediate experience simply is what it is. Truth and falsity only enter the scene when we raise questions about the *meaning* of experience:

> Truth and falsity are not properties of any experience or thing, in and of it-self or in its first intention; *but of things where the problem of assurance consciously enters in. Truth and falsity present themselves as significant facts only in situations in which specific meanings are intentionally compared and contrasted with reference to the question of worth, as to the reliability of meaning.* (Dewey 1906b, 118, emphasis in original)

Truth and falsity are therefore not concerned with paper as such, but with the *relationship* between our experience of paper on the one hand and our possible actions or responses on the other. We approach paper as if we can write on it; the piece of paper *means* "being able to write on it." But it is only when we act that we can know whether this inferred meaning can become actual—or, in more day-to-day terms, whether what we expected the situation to be was indeed the case. This not only means that "truth" is always contextual and related to action, it also means that truth is itself *temporal*. Truth does not refer to an alleged correspondence between a proposition and reality. It has to do with the correspondence between *suggested* meaning and *realized* meaning, that is, meaning "put into practice": "The agreement, correspondence, is between purpose, plan, and its own execution, fulfillment" (Dewey 1907a, 84).

This account does not mean that truth becomes disconnected from reality. The contrary is the case, not only because of the transactional framework that lies behind Dewey's theory of knowledge, but also because of the intervention of action, really, the *indispensable* role of action in the process that results in knowledge. This means that knowledge is not a passive registration of reality "out there." Our intervention, our action, is a crucial, necessary, and constitutive part of knowledge. In this sense we can say that knowledge is always a human construction, just as the objects of knowledge are (we will return to this theme in chapter 4). But this does not mean that anything is possible. We always intervene in an existing course of events, and, although our intervention introduces change, it will always be change of an existing course of events. We cannot create *ex nihilo*, we cannot construct out of nothing. The only possible construction is a *re*construction.

CONCLUSION

In this chapter we have presented the main "building blocks" of Dewey's theory of knowledge. As we have noted several times, one of the main difficulties with understanding Dewey's approach is that he used many of the concepts of the philosophical tradition in a new and different way. As long as one reads Dewey with habits of mind that were formed in the context of the very philosophical tradition that Dewey was criticizing, one will almost definitely miss the originality and distinctiveness of Dewey's position.

We have noted this problem in Dewey's use of the concept of "experience." For Dewey "experience" refers to the transaction of organism and environment; it is not some mysterious inner mental event or a passive "sensing" of the world. It is for precisely this reason that Dewey could present experience as the means of penetrating continually further into the heart of nature. Yet, and this is another important but easily overseen aspect of Dewey's position, while experience secures that we are "in touch" with nature, experience itself is, as such, not (yet) knowledge. The "missing link" between experience and knowledge is action, because it is only through action that we can get an understanding of the conditions of the *happening* of an experience. Further, as we will discuss in more detail in chapter 3, knowledge only becomes *conscious* knowledge, knowledge "of," when reflection is introduced in the transformation of transaction. Taken together, this results in a *temporal* theory of knowledge.

The final point that we want to make in this chapter is that for Dewey it is not only knowledge that has a temporal character. He also claimed that reality itself should be understood in temporal terms. It is not simply a matter of human action introducing an element of change in a universe that is ultimately static and permanent. Dewey argued that reality itself is "dynamic and self-evolving" (1903b, 296). The "essential contrast," as he put it, "is that reality . . . for pragmatism is still in the making" (1908a, 99). Knowing, on this account, is not something that comes from "the outside" but is part of reality-in-change. It is "reality making a particular and specified sort of change" (Dewey 1908b, 129).

One of the most important implications of this understanding of reality is that the domain of the "practical" is released from its secondary status: It is a domain of potential inquiry and knowledge as much as any other. "In current philosophy," Dewey wrote in 1908, "everything of a practical nature is regarded as merely personal, and the merely has the force of denying legitimate standing in the court of cosmic jurisdiction" (1908b, 126). But such relegation of "need, of stress and strain, strife and satisfaction" to the merely personal is nothing but a "thoughtless rehearsal of ancestral prejudice" (Dewey 1908b, 126–27). Dewey suggested that the reason that the practical was given a lower status in Western philosophy than the theoretical was *not* because reality is ultimately static. The argument went precisely the other way around: Because the practical had a lower status than the theoretical, Greek philosophers assumed that "real" reality could not be the reality of practical life but had to be the static reality of the life of theory. In a sense, Dewey simply started at the other end of the equation by taking *change, and not immutability,* as the measure of reality.

It is important to see here that Dewey was *not* arguing for shifting the attention from the building blocks of reality to the interaction between these building blocks. Such a view, which relies on the assumption that "only a permanent can change and that change is alteration of a permanent" (Dewey 1908b, 141), still doesn't take change seriously enough. It still denies "temporal quality to reality as such" (Dewey 1925a, 119) and keeps looking for a reality "behind" the ever-changing world to explain change. This would still entail a "metaphysics of *essence*." Dewey, on the other hand, was articulating a "metaphysics of *existence*" (1929a, 163), in which every existence is simply an event (and not a material "thing"). This is what lies behind the idea of *transaction*, "where systems of description and naming are employed to deal with aspects and phases of action, without final attribution to elements or other presumptively detachable or independent entities, essences, or realities" (Dewey and Bentley 1949, 101–2). This view is intimately connected with the claim that knowing is a form of doing, a transaction in and of reality. As long as we think that reality is ultimately static, the idea that knowing is doing leads to the conclusion that knowledge is not possible. In Dewey's own words,

> If we persist in the traditional conception, according to which the thing to be known is something which exists prior to and wholly apart from the act of knowing, then discovery of the fact that the act of observation, necessary in existential knowing, modifies that preexisting something, is proof that the act of knowing gets in its own way, frustrating its own intent. (Dewey 1929a, 164)

But if reality can undergo change *without* thereby ceasing to be real, then "there can be no *formal* bar to knowing being one specific kind of change in things, nor to its test being found in the successful carrying into effect of the kind of change intended " (Dewey 1908b, 129). In that case it is our old conception of knowledge as a (static) picture of a (static) reality that simply has to go. "[I]f all existences are in transition, then the knowledge which treats them as if they were something of which knowledge is a kodak fixation is just the kind of knowledge which refracts and perverts them" (Dewey 1908b, 129).

The metaphysics of existence, in other words, reveals both why knowing as "the conversion of undirected changes into changes directed toward an intended conclusion" (Dewey 1929a, 163) is *necessary*, and why it is *possible* (Sleeper 1986, 61). This, in turn, makes clear why Dewey rejected the idea that we should first have a metaphysics and develop our understanding of knowing and coming to know after that. For Dewey it is knowing, it is the process of inquiry, that should shape our concept of being, and not vice versa (Sleeper 1986, 61).

3

The Process of Inquiry

> [S]cientific results furnish a rule for the conduct of *observations and inquiries,* not a rule for overt action.
>
> —John Dewey (1929b, 15)

In chapter 2 we presented Dewey's temporal theory of knowledge, a theory that is intimately connected with his temporal metaphysics of existence. Dewey rejected the idea of an original separation of subject and object. He also rejected the related idea of knowledge as a mirroring of an eternal, static reality. Instead he took his point of departure in the ever-changing organism-environment transaction. Knowing is not outside of this process but part of it. While experience concerns transaction "as it is," knowledge has to do with the value or meaning of experience. One of Dewey's central insights is that the only way in which we can find out the meaning of immediate experience is by means of action. In this respect we can say that knowledge results from the cooperation of experience and action. The move from trial-and-error action to intelligent action is effected by the insertion of *reflection*, which takes place by means of language. One implication of Dewey's approach is that we only know the world as a result of our actions. Another major implication is that knowledge is always concerned with the antecedents and consequences of experience and not with experience itself. In this respect we can say that knowledge itself is always temporal.

In this chapter we want to take a closer look at the process of the acquisition of knowledge, which is what Dewey refers to as *inquiry*.

Dewey's theory of the process of inquiry is not an a priori prescriptive theory of how inquiry should proceed or how knowledge should be acquired. It is, rather, a *reconstructive* theory, an attempt to articulate the *logic* of the cognitive mode of experience, the way in which the cognitive model actually operates. Dewey's reconstructive view not only implies that an understanding of the "logic" of inquiry should come from an examination of actual processes of inquiry; he took the even stronger position that the forms of logic, the principles and methods we use in the acquisition of knowledge, *originate* in operations of inquiry (Dewey 1938a, 11) and have no status beyond their proven efficacy for human purposes. They are "ways of treating subject-matter that have been found so determinative of sound conclusions in the past that they are taken to regulate further inquiry until definitive grounds are found for questioning them" (Dewey 1938a, 21).

Dewey's position here entails a rejection of the distinction between, on the one hand, a normative or prescriptive *logic* of inquiry and, on the other hand, an empirical or descriptive *methodology* of inquiry (Dewey 1938a, 13). It is not that philosophy can first tell us what valid knowledge is and then, on that basis, we simply devise our methods for the acquisition of knowledge accordingly. Just as our understanding of knowledge (the cognitive mode of experience) can only come from a reconstruction of actual processes of knowledge acquisition, so can our methods of inquiry only be criticized, improved, and validated in and through the process of inquiry itself.

In this respect the "art of knowing" does not differ from other arts, such as the art of metallurgy: "Is there any reason," Dewey asked, "to suppose that advance in the art of metallurgy has been due to application of an external standard?" According to Dewey this is not the case: "The 'norms' used at present have developed out of the processes by which metallic ores were formerly treated. . . . [S]ome procedures worked; some succeeded in reaching the end intended; others failed. The latter were dropped; the former were retained and extended" (Dewey 1938a, 14).

In the first section of this chapter we discuss Dewey's theory of the process of inquiry. We outline the general structure of this process and discuss some of the most salient features of Dewey's understanding of this process. Against this background, we then pay attention to the differences between inquiry into the natural and the social domains. Finally, we take a closer look at the specific nature of educational inquiry. In the course of this chapter we also comment on the distinction between the words *inquiry* and *research*. To put it briefly, inquiry refers to all processes of intelligent experimental problem solving, while research denotes the deliberate instigation of intelligent experimental problem solving in order to generate knowledge and understanding.

THE THEORY OF INQUIRY

Dewey maintains that knowledge can be rightly understood "only in connection with considerations of time and temporal position" (1916b, 336). This claim entails more than the rather trivial observation that the process of inquiry takes time. The temporal quality of inquiry means "that the objective subject-matter of inquiry undergoes temporal modification" (Dewey 1938a, 122). We should therefore understand inquiry as a *serial or sequential* process. The serial or sequential nature of inquiry is rooted in the conditions of life itself. Inquiry does not solve problems by returning to a previous, stable situation, but by means of a transformation of the current situation into a *new* situation. There is, therefore, no absolute end to inquiry. It is not that there will be a point at which we can know everything that there is to know, even if that were possible, because every settlement of a situation institutes *new* conditions that, in turn, occasion *new* problems (Dewey 1938a, 42), and the cycle begins again.

The serial or sequential nature of inquiry clearly comes to the fore in Dewey's reconstruction of inquiry as a process that consists of several steps or stages. Throughout his work we can find several slightly different descriptions of these steps (see, for example, 1916a, 157–58; 1922c, 61; 1933, 190–209). The earliest formulation dates from 1909 and describes the process as follows: "(i) A felt difficulty, (ii) its location and definition, (iii) suggestion of possible solution, (iv) development by reasoning of the bearings of the suggestion, (v) further observation and experiment leading to its acceptance or rejection" (1909a, 246–37). The analysis of the process of inquiry as a series of steps or stages is not meant to say that actual inquiries always follow or should follow this exact pattern. The reconstruction is only meant to identify the logical development of an act of inquiry. It is a matter of indifference which component actually comes first. Not even the occurrence of a problem need come absolutely first in time (Dewey 1922c, 62; see also below).

Indeterminate and Problematic Situations

We have already seen that the "natural" starting point for inquiry is the situation in which there are conflicting habits, the situation in which we do not "know" how to respond. In such a situation there is "uncertainty as to the *what* of the experience together with the certainty *that* there is such an experience" (Dewey 1903b, 330). One of the recurring questions in Dewey's discussion of the process of inquiry is whether what evokes inquiry—the conflict of habits—should itself be seen as part of the process of inquiry. Does inquiry only start *after* the disruption of coordinated transaction? Or is the disruption the first step of the process? This question may seem academic, but it does make sense when it is acknowledged that inquiry—the process in which reflection and action cooperate in order to restore coordination—is only one of the ways in which coordination can be restored. Trial and error or a fortunate change in the environing conditions are other ways in which this can be achieved.

Dewey solved the problem by introducing a distinction between *indeterminate* and *problematic* situations. Conflicting habits constitute an *indeterminate* situation. Although this is a necessary condition for the transformation of experience into cognitive experience, the indeterminate situation is itself not cognitive. It is simply a natural event. It is only when such a situation is identified as a *problematic* situation that inquiry begins and experience turns into the cognitive mode. A teacher may feel uneasy about what is happening in her classroom, and as a result may be distracted or find it difficult to focus. The normal "flow" of teaching is, in a sense, disrupted. For Dewey this would count as an *indeterminate* situation. As soon as the teacher acknowledges that something needs to be done, that the source of the uneasiness should be identified, the indeterminate situation turns into a problematic situation. It is here that inquiry begins. As Dewey put it: "To see that a situation requires inquiry is the initial step in inquiry" (1938a, 111).

Dewey's distinction between indeterminate and problematic situations is reflected in the following, slightly different, description of the stages of the process of inquiry: "(i) The occurrence of a problem; (ii) its specification; (iii) occurrence of a solving suggestion or supposition, hypothesis; (iv) elaboration of suggestions, or reasoning; (v) experimental testing" (1922c, 61).

Dewey's distinction between indeterminate and problematic situations reveals that his theory of inquiry does not rely on an "objectivistic" understanding of what problems are. Problems are not simply "there" but emerge as a result of the identification of an indeterminate situation *as* being problematic, *as* being in need of inquiry. After all, the teacher does not yet know what the problem is. That is precisely what needs to be found out. A similar remark can be made about indeterminate situations. What is indeterminate is not some state of affairs "outside" and independent of the human organism. The indeterminateness concerns the organism-environment *transaction*. *Situation* is the word Dewey used to refer to this transaction. This implies that similar external conditions do not necessarily lead to similar indeterminate situations. What is unclear and confusing for one person is not necessarily also unclear and confusing for another person. All depends upon the *relationship* between environing conditions and available habits.

Conceptual and Existential Operations

The notion of the indeterminate situation plays a central role in Dewey's definition of inquiry. He writes, *"Inquiry is the controlled or directed transformation of an indeterminate situation into one that is so determinate in its constituent distinctions and relations as to convert the elements of the original situation into a unified whole"* (1938a, 108; emphasis in original). This definition emphasizes once more that inquiry is not a mental process, not something that happens in the human mind, but that it is the actual transformation of a situation—where a situation always denotes the transaction of organism and environment. What distinguishes inquiry from trial and error is the fact that the transformation of the situation is *controlled* or *directed* by means of reflection or thinking. The process of inquiry thus consists of the cooperation of two kinds of operations: *existential operations* (the actual transformation of the situation) and *conceptual operations* (reflection or thinking). In some phases of the process of inquiry, the emphasis will be on conceptual operations, while in other phases the existential operations will be more prominent. But it is always the cooperation of the two operations and never only one of them. If our teacher would only think about the situation, without doing anything (including not changing her own behavior), the indeterminateness of the situation would remain. If, on the other hand, the teacher would act without trying to understand, it would be a case of trial and error, of hit and miss, which may be successful, but which would not add to any understanding and for that reason would not count as an example of inquiry.

One purpose of conceptual operations is to develop suggestions for possible lines of action. But conceptual operations are also needed to suggest possible constituents and causes of the indeterminate situation. Conceptual operations not only guide the eventual transformation of the indeterminate situation into a determinate situation, they also provide guidance for intermediate activities such as observation.

While indeterminate situations in a sense simply "happen," the process of inquiry begins when we try to identify what is actually happening. In a sense this is all there is to know, because as soon as we know the "history" of the indeterminate situation, that is, its antecedents and constituents, we hold the key to solving the problem. Not only is it true that "a problem well put is half-solved" (Dewey 1938a, 112), in fact, we only know what the problem is at the very moment that we are able to solve it: "Problem and solution stand out *completely* at the same time" (Dewey 1933, 201).

Facts and Ideas

Finding out what actually is problematic about the indeterminate situation is, therefore, a crucial moment in the process of inquiry. The first step toward the identification of the problem lies in the collection of *facts*. This is not just anything that might be collected at a given moment in time; we need to find the constituents of the indeterminate situation, constituents which themselves are not indeterminate. Dewey called these constituents the *facts of the case*. The facts of the case "constitute the terms of the problem, because they are the conditions that must be reckoned with or taken account of in any relevant solution that is proposed" (Dewey 1938a, 113).

In order to find the facts of the case we need observation. But not everything we observe will be a possible fact of the case. Everything depends on the ideas we have about the possible nature of the problem. Ideas, in other words, give direction to our observations, just as they give meaning to what we observe: "A color seen at a particular locus in a spectral band is, for example, of immense intellectual importance in chemistry and in astro-physics. But *merely* as seen, as a bare sensory quality, it is the same for the clodhopper and the scientist; it is just and only another color the eye has happened upon" (Dewey 1929a, 91). This means that facts and ideas do not develop independently but that there is a constant "check" between the two. When the facts of the case become clearer, it becomes possible to formulate more precise ideas about how to transform the situation. When we have more precise ideas about what might solve the problem, this in turn gives more focus and direction to our observations. It could be that the teacher from our example assumes that the disruption of the teaching situation has to do with the particular behavior of one particular student. This would focus her attention on this student. We could say that it is a hypothesis about the problem that guides her observation. She may then try to find out what it is about this student that makes her feel uneasy, that interrupts the natural flow of her teaching. Such a question leads to further investigation, further observation, further questions, and so on. Gradually the teacher might move to a better understanding of what the problem is, and hence to ideas about how it might be addressed.

In the process of inquiry ideas usually start their career as suggestions. Since suggestions are only vague, they need further development. The development of suggested meanings—reasoning—is needed in order to achieve an idea of the possible meaning of what is being observed. It is precisely at this point that previously acquired knowledge enters into the process of inquiry, since it provides a network of possible conceptual operations, a network, moreover, which has proven to be successful in the past. Although there is no guarantee that "old" knowledge will be successful for the solution of the problem at hand, it can at least suggest a variety of different approaches for understanding the situation, interpreting observations, and possible action. The use of "old" knowledge is one way in which our inquiry—and hence our action more generally—can become more intelligent. Our teacher may come to the conclusion that the student is not paying attention to her teaching and that her feeling of uneasiness has to do with the fact that this student usually is full of attention. This simple conclusion is only the first step, because the question then is why the student is not paying attention. There can be many causes for this, and a good teacher may well have an internal checklist of possible causes. Is the teaching not interesting? Is the student tired? Could there be problems at home? If the teacher wants to address the problem adequately, she needs to rely on her knowledge—and maybe more specialist knowledge—in order to direct her further investigation and action.

As long as the transformation of the indeterminate situation into a determinate situation has not taken place, both facts and ideas only have a provisional status:

> The selection of what is relevant to the characterization of the problem and the projection of the method of dealing with it are theoretic, hypothetic, intellectual—that is, they are tentative ways of viewing the matter for the sake of guiding, economizing and freeing the activities through which it may *really* be dealt with. (Dewey 1907b, 73)

Facts, like ideas, must therefore be *represented* by means of symbols, because it is only in this way that facts can be manipulated and experimented
with. In order to make the distinction between symbolized (possible) facts
and (actual) facts of the case, Dewey referred to the first as *data*.

Since both facts and ideas only have a provisional status as long as the
situation is not transformed into a determinate situation, the difference between them is also provisional—or to be more precise: The distinction between facts and ideas is a functional distinction that doesn't correspond
with any distinction in "reality." Dewey explains,

> [P]erceptual and conceptual materials are instituted in functional correlativ-
> ity with each other, in such a manner that the former locates and describes
> the problem while the latter represents a possible method of solution. Both
> are determinations in and by inquiry of the original problematic situation
> whose pervasive quality controls their institutions and their contents. Both
> are finally checked by their capacity to work together to introduce a re-
> solved unified situation. (Dewey 1938a, 115)

The distinction between facts and ideas, therefore, does *not* coincide with
the distinction between conceptual and existential operations. The distinction between facts and ideas lies wholly on the conceptual "side" of
the process of inquiry. The teacher of our example will have ideas about
what is "the case" (facts) and ideas about ways of addressing the problem
(ideas)—but for the moment both the facts and the ideas are only ideas,
only hypotheses, only assumptions.

Functional Correspondence

In chapter 2 we discussed how inference plays a central role in Dewey's
understanding of knowledge. We defined inference as a reaction to something that is distant in time or place. The inferential act, to use Dewey's
own words, "consists in taking up an attitude of response to an absent
thing as if it were present" (1915b, 70).

In the context of his discussion of the process of inquiry Dewey emphasized that inference is an *existential* relationship. It is a cloud meaning
rain; it is smoke meaning fire. The present cloud, so we could say, is a *sign*
for the not-yet present rain. Dewey referred to this representative relationship as *significance*. Signs like these ("natural signs") exist in an actual "spatial-temporal context" and hence provide evidence of the existence of something else. While signs have a representative capacity, this

capacity is highly restricted, for it only exists under limited conditions. The situation completely changes, however, when the *meaning* "smoke" is embodied in an existence, like a word-sound or a mark on paper. In this case the meaning is liberated with respect to its representative function. It can then be related to other meanings in a language-system; not only to the meaning of "fire" but also to such apparently unrelated meanings as "friction, changes of temperature, oxygen, molecular constitution, and, by intervening meaning-symbols, to the laws of thermodynamics" (Dewey 1938a, 58). Dewey called the representative relationship between symbols *implication*. The strength of symbols is that they have a much more flexible and much more encompassing representative capacity. What they lack is that they do not provide evidence of any existence. The only way in which symbols and signs can be connected is by means of existential operations. According to Dewey there is no "automatic" one-to-one correspondence of symbols and existential objects. The only way in which we can establish a connection between the two is by means of action. Without the intervention of a specific kind of existential operation, symbols "cannot indicate or discriminate the *objects* to which they refer" (Dewey 1938a, 60). To put it simply: It is only when our teacher acts on her ideas about what is the case and how the problem could be addressed, that a relationship between her ideas (about the facts and about the possible solutions) and the actual situation is established.

With the help of these distinctions we can now describe the process of inquiry in detail. The starting point is the indeterminate situation, which is a transaction in which coordination cannot be accomplished. What we need is knowledge of the antecedents of the situation, so that an adequate response can occur. What we need to know, in other words, is the *significance* of the indeterminate situation. The only way in which coordination can be restored is by means of appropriate action. In order to find the most appropriate line of action we need to formulate suggestions about the possible causes of the situation. These suggestions (*meanings*) can first be developed on a conceptual level (*implication*). On the basis of this we can act in or on the situation and then observe the consequences of our actions. This will give us (new) *facts* that can be symbolized so that they can be entered into the conceptual development of a possible solution. In this process facts become *data*. The cooperation of data and ideas results in a proposal for action: the *hypothesis*. The hypothesis articulates a relationship between actions and consequences on the basis of a hypothetical interpretation of what is problematic about the indeterminate situation.

Whether the suggested relations (implications) correspond with the actual connections can only be found out by means of acting out the suggested line of action. If the action indeed has the expected result (that is, coordinated action), a unified situation has been created. If not, there is more to be learned.

It is of crucial importance to see that the correspondence between the relations between symbols (inference), on the one hand, and the actual connections (significance) that are brought about by means of acting, on the other, is a strictly *functional* correspondence. When our actions indeed bring about a unified situation, this does not mean that the relationships on a conceptual level are identical with the relationships on an existential level. The only thing that can be concluded is that the conclusions reached on a conceptual level are doing what they ought to do in bringing about a unified situation. We could say that the conceptual operations lead to the same outcome as the existential operations. But this does not mean that all the elements of the conceptual operations and their relations are in any way identical with the elements of the existential situation and the way in which they interrelate. Although successful inquiry brings about a correspondence between "symbols" and "existence" or "language" and "reality"—or, to be more precise, between *conceptual operations* and *existential operations*—the correspondence is only a functional one. How should we understand this? Our teacher may have come to the conclusion that her uneasiness was caused by the fact that what she was teaching was in no way a challenge for her student, because the level at which she tried to teach it was far below what the student had already achieved. The solution she found, then, was to adjust her teaching in such a way that it related much better to the expectations and background knowledge of this particular student. When she did so, the student did indeed pay attention, and the flow of teaching was reestablished. Now, while the inquiry conducted by the teacher has come to a successful conclusion—the transformation of an indeterminate transaction into a determinate transaction— this does not mean that the hypotheses and mini-theories she developed in this process tell us what the situation "out there" was really like. The successful conclusion of this inquiry only proves that the ideas developed during the process were effective in transforming the situation from an indeterminate into a determinate one.

If we would think of the process of inquiry as a procedure for testing the validity or worth of our conceptual operations (our "theorizing" and "reasoning"), then the question cannot be whether our theories and the conceptual operations we perform on the basis of our theories are *identical* with the real world of existential operations and connections. The only relevant question is whether our conceptual operations do what we expect them to do. Precisely for this reason—and this is a crucial point in understanding the way in which pragmatism differs from common ways of understanding the relationship between theory or language and reality—it is a mistake to assume that a successful existential operation would prove the *truth* of the conceptual operations (theories, propositions, hypotheses, and so on). The conceptual operations, the propositions and hypotheses that we use, are nothing but means in a process that aims at restoring coordinated action. Just as it makes no sense to ask whether a hammer is true or false—means or instruments are neither true nor false but are simply more or less adequate to do what we expect them to do—it also makes no sense to ask whether our theories or propositions and hypotheses are true or false. As Dewey put it: "[T]ruth-falsity is *not* a property of propositions" (1938a, 287).

The Outcome of the Process of Inquiry

The process of inquiry comes to an end when a unified situation is established. In a sense we could say that the occurrence of a unified situation proves that the inference was correct or *warranted*. It becomes clear, in other words, that it was indeed possible to act on experience x as meaning y.

In chapter 2 we showed how it is possible to restore coordinated transaction on a strictly habitual level, that is, by means of trial and error. What is special about the process of inquiry is that the (habitual) existential operations are in a sense "embedded" in a conceptual network. Because of this, the process of inquiry has a double outcome: There is not only a change in the habits of the organism, but also a change in the relationship between symbols, or in other words, a new *meaning*. After all, if it has been proven that we can act on x as meaning y, then this means—on the conceptual level—that x now also has y as one of its possible meanings. In terms of our example: A student not paying attention now also has "not being sufficiently challenged" as one of the situation's possible meanings. It is in this way that our conceptual networks, our theories, emerge and develop over time. These networks and theories can be seen as storage depots of the outcomes of inquiries in that they specify possible relationships between symbols, relationships that have shown to be possible in the past. The more refined these networks become, the more refined—and presumably the more sophisticated and hopefully more successful—the conceptual operations in actual processes of inquiry can be.

Dewey's analysis of the process of inquiry as the cooperation of existential and conceptual operations clearly shows that it is precisely because of this cooperation that inquiry has both an "actual" and a "conceptual" outcome. Although conceptual operations are as such not necessary to bring about a unified situation—because this can also happen through trial and error—they are necessary if we want to *learn* something from solving the problems we encounter. Without conceptual operations, without reasoning or thinking, our problem solving remains haphazard and unintelligent. Existential operations are indispensable, not only to bring about a unified situation but also in order to find out the value and worth of our ideas. Without implications for action our ideas—that is both our ideas about the facts of the case and our ideas about necessary lines of action—remain merely ideas.

In some of his writings Dewey referred to the conceptual outcome of inquiry as *knowledge*—and this may indeed be close to the way in which we are inclined to use that word in our day-to-day speech. Yet from a more technical or philosophical point of view, there are several problems with the concept. One is that the word *knowledge* evokes associations with the epistemological tradition in which it is claimed that something only counts as knowledge if it conforms to preestablished criteria of what knowledge is, what counts as knowledge. We have seen that Dewey rejected the possibility that we can say anything *general* about what knowledge is apart from its being the outcome of inquiry. For this reason Dewey's use of the word *knowledge* is, strictly speaking, tautological: "That which satisfactorily terminates inquiry is, by definition knowledge; it is knowledge because it *is* the appropriate close of inquiry" (Dewey 1938a, 15).

A further problem with using the word *knowledge* to describe the outcome of inquiry is that it may seem as if the outcome of inquiry is definitive; that knowledge as knowledge is certain and definitive for now and forever. The conceptual outcome of inquiry is, however, always related to the specific situation in which it was achieved. Knowledge in this account is always provisional. The settlement of a particular situation by a particular inquiry is no guarantee that that conclusion will always remain settled. Dewey emphasized that there is no belief so settled as not to be exposed to further inquiry. In every new case we can ask the question whether any conclusions reached in the past still hold. This does not mean, of course, that every conclusion reached should be put into question in every new situation. This would be impossible. The problem is also that we cannot doubt everything at the same time. We need some ground to stand on in order to put something else into question.

For all of these reasons Dewey preferred to use the expression *warranted assertion* to denote the *conceptual* outcome of inquiry, rather than *knowledge*, let alone *true knowledge* or *truth*. (The existential outcome, as we have already seen, is called the unified or determined situation.) Another reason for preferring the expression *warranted assertion* is that it expresses more clearly the relationship with concrete processes of inquiry. Assertions are always only warranted in relation to concrete inquiries. Whether they retain their value in other inquiries is something that cannot be known beforehand, but which has to be established again and again in every new inquiry.

From Inquiry to Research

The transformation of an indeterminate situation into a determinate situation is the natural occasion for the process of inquiry and, therefore, for the transition of experience into the cognitive mode. But this does not imply, of course, that we can only acquire knowledge through the solution of problems. In a sense, Dewey's only claim is that we do acquire knowledge, we do learn something about the relationship between our actions and their consequences, when we solve the problems we encounter in an active, experimental, and reflective manner. But there is no need to wait for the occurrence of indeterminate situations in order to inquire into such relationships. Systematic inquiry into actions and consequences can also be conducted deliberately and independent of problem-solving activities. Dewey argued that there are even people who have made their profession out of this, namely, researchers or scientists, "a body of persons working at knowing as another body is working at farming or engineering" (1915b, 65).

Although inquiry is meant to bring about the existential transformation of an indeterminate situation into a unified situation, this does not mean that when inquiry is taken out of the context of problem solving, existential transformations (action) no longer play a role. First of all, one might say that the process of research often involves *creating* an indeterminate situation, or seeking one out, for the sake of advancing knowledge. Further, following Dewey's transactional approach, it is the case that we need action in order to determine the meaning of the conceptual operations in the process of inquiry. Action is the process through which ideas are transformed into knowledge—or, in Dewey's vocabulary, to transform hypotheses into warranted assertions. Dewey emphasized that if we would exclude acting on an idea, "no conceivable amount or kind of intellectualistic procedure can confirm or refute the idea, or throw any light upon its validity" (1907a, 85). Acting on the basis of suggested meanings is therefore the "only conceivable verification of the intellectual factors" (Dewey 1907b, 66).

Meaning, Verification, and Truth

Dewey used the word *verification* in this context in a strictly literal sense, namely, as the *activity* of making something true (Dewey 1907b, 66). What is made true in the process of verification are our inferences, that is, our ideas about the relationship between our actions and their consequences in a transactional situation. When we act on the basis of what we assume that the current experience will result in when acted on (inference), and this is indeed what happens, we can say that our inference has been made true. In our example: Our teacher inferred that when she would change her teaching to make it more challenging for this particular student, the student would pay attention. Given that her change of teaching indeed changed the student's attitude, we can say that this inference was made true through the teacher's inquiry.

This can, as we have discussed in chapter 2, occur strictly on the level of habits. In the process of inquiry, however, we develop our inference first through conceptual operations (reasoning) and then choose our actions on the basis of the outcome of such operations. If we are successful in creating a unified situation, we can also say that our ideas are made true, albeit in the specific (temporal) sense in which truth means "fulfillment of the consequences to which an idea . . . refers" (Dewey 1911a, 56). We should keep this temporal focus in mind so as not to forget that the correspondence between "ideas" and "reality" is a *functional* correspondence. Ideas, as Dewey explains, "are anticipated consequences (forecasts) of what will happen when certain operations are executed under and with respect to observed conditions" (1938a, 113).

For Dewey, therefore, truth is not about the correspondence between descriptions of reality and reality itself. The correspondence, in other words, is not static or descriptive. For Dewey the correspondence is active and temporal; it is included in the cycle of action-reflection-action. To "verify," for Dewey, therefore does not mean to establish that a statement about how reality "is" is indeed as reality "is"—to verify an idea means that the relation between actions and consequences specified in the idea has actually happened. The key to understanding Dewey, in other words, is to get away from the idea that knowledge is a picture of reality; knowledge, for Dewey, is something we use in order to live, work, and act in the world.

Taken together, the foregoing remarks imply that the acquisition of knowledge independent of the context of problem solving can be understood as a process of the acquisition of meanings. There is no fundamental difference between the way in which we acquire meanings in the context of problem solving and outside of such a context. In both cases the intervention of action in order to establish the value of our inferences is crucial. The main reason why it makes sense to acquire meanings—that is, to look for possible relationships between actions and consequences—is that these relationships, when symbolized (for example, as theories) can be used in future problem-solving inquiries. After all, the conceptual component of the process of inquiry is not only meant to raise the process above the level of blind trial and error; it also allows for the introduction of the outcomes of previous processes of inquiry into current problem-solving processes. This, as we have seen, constitutes the crucial difference between (mere) action and intelligent action. Dewey described it as follows:

> [A]ttained knowledge produces *meanings* and . . . these meanings are capable of being separated from the special cases of knowledge in which they originally appear and of being incorporated and funded cumulatively in habits so as to constitute . . . *intelligence* when actually applied in new experiences. (1939b, 48; emphasis in original)

One of the implications of this idea is that there is a direct relationship between the amount of "old" knowledge or meaning that an individual can have access to and the opportunities for an intelligent approach to problematic situations. This is first of all true on an intra-individual level. The more numerous and varied our previous experiences and our previous knowledge and learning are, the more sophisticated our conceptual operations will be and the better chance we will have of finding an adequate way of dealing with the problems we encounter. This, as Dewey would put it, is the decisive difference between an intelligent and an unintelligent actor. But the same logic holds on an inter-individual level. The more we can share in the experiences of others, the more resources we will have for dealing with our problems, and hence the more intelligent our collective problem solving will be (or at least can be). Precisely along these lines Dewey saw a strong and intimate connection between his theory of knowledge and his political philosophy. He writes, "[S]ince democracy stands in principle for free interchange, for social continuity, it must develop a theory of knowledge which sees in knowledge the method by which one experience is made available in giving direction and meaning to another" (1916a, 354–55).

There is an important implication for research in this line of thought. Many would argue that research simply is a systematic form of inquiry—and Dewey would not object to such a definition. In a sense, his definition of researchers says nothing more than that some people conduct inquiries for a living. What is important about research, however, is that it is conducted in the open, that it is made totally transparent, so that others (researchers, but not only researchers) can follow critically how the conclusions of a particular inquiry have been reached. Research, in the words of Lawrence Stenhouse, is *systematic inquiry made public* (1983, 185).

Against this background it is important to note that the use of the outcomes of previous processes of inquiry is not—or not exclusively—to be thought of as the *application* of existing knowledge. As such it is natural that the outcomes of specific processes of inquiry, the warranted assertions we make on the basis of such processes, become more and more detached from the contexts in which they first emerged and (almost) start to lead a life of their own. What was the fallible outcome of one process of inquiry can become an almost infallible fact when used in another situation. Dewey observed that this is what often happens in research, where one research project builds on the outcomes of a previous one and, in doing so, gives these outcomes more status and certainty than they initially had. While this is conceivable if not common practice in how we develop our knowledge and understanding of the world, Dewey warned that we should not think of this as simply or exclusively the application of secure and certain knowledge in new situations: "When applied to new cases, used as resources for coping with new difficulties, the oldest of truths are to some extent remade. Indeed it is only through such application and such remaking that truths retain their freshness and validity" (1907b, 74). In this sense we could say that application is part of the process of continuous verification. Although researchers can try to produce "facts" that are as stable and secure as possible in the context in which they are produced, the real verification happens again and again in the new contexts in which these "facts" are being used or applied. Hence Dewey concluded that the "widest possible range of application is the means of the deepest verification" (1915b, 82). For this reason we can think of verification as ultimately a *social* process (Dewey 1911b, 77). When we apply existing knowledge in new situations, the question of success is not only one of the applicability of that knowledge in this situation; it is also a test of whether the knowledge holds under new circumstances. Both issues are always at the same time at stake in the use of existing knowledge for dealing with new problems.

Inquiry and the Cycle of Empirical Research

Dewey's description of the process of inquiry comes very close to our everyday understanding of how we deal with problems. When we don't know what to do, or how to respond, we try to find out what the problem is, we develop a strategy for dealing with it, and we try out the strategy. If we are successful we can not only claim to have found a solution for the problem; it also suggests that our understanding of the problem was "correct"—or at least adequate. When we abstract from the actual context of problem solving and think of the process of inquiry as a process of the acquisition of knowledge, it is again not too difficult to recognize the main components of experimental empirical research. Our point of departure is a hypothesis about what might be the case. We develop an experimental strategy in order to investigate the situation. We perform experiment(s) and observe results. On the basis of this we draw our conclusions.

Although Dewey's description of the process of inquiry may look familiar, both in terms of everyday problem solving and in terms of the cycle of experimental empirical research, it is important to keep in mind that behind all this lies a very specific set of assumptions. Dewey's discussion of the process of inquiry should be understood not only in terms of his transactional approach, but also as an expression of his temporal metaphysics of existence and his temporal theory of knowledge. We should not forget, in other words, that when a process of inquiry results in a warranted assertion, this assertion is not a description about how the world out there is, but is always a description of a relationship between our actions and their consequences. It is for precisely this reason that Dewey's

ideas about the process of inquiry and about the experimental acquisition
of knowledge differ fundamentally from the interpretations given by pos-
itivists *and* by postpositivists. Although Dewey has often been included in
the postpositivist "canon" (see Phillips and Burbules 2000), we believe
that this should be done extremely cautiously—and perhaps not even at
all. After all, Dewey's ideas rely on a completely different metaphysics
and a completely different theory of knowledge, which, as we have
shown, is not even an *epistemology* in the traditional sense of the word.

We will return to the wider implications of the special position Dewey
took in chapter 4. Before we do that, we want to say a few words about
inquiry in the social domain and, more specifically, educational inquiry.

NATURAL INQUIRY AND SOCIAL INQUIRY

In our discussion so far the distinction between inquiry into the natural domain and inquiry into the social domain has hardly played a role. There
are at least two reasons why this distinction does not figure prominently
in Dewey's pragmatism.

The first reason is of an ontological nature and has to do with Dewey's
rejection of the idea that the universe consists of two completely different
"substances"—mind and matter. Dewey's naturalistic approach claims
that there is a continuity between the material world and the world of consciousness, meaning, interaction and communication. When Dewey therefore argued that "[t]he subject-matter of social problems is existential"
and that in the broad sense of "natural," social sciences are "branches of
natural science" (1938a, 481), he is not proposing a materialistic reductionism in which only what can be stated in the language of physics can
be deemed real. He only wanted to remind us of the *continuity* between
the natural and the social world. In "the social," Dewey explained, "the
physical is taken up into a wider and more complex and delicate system
of interactions so that it takes on new properties by release of potentialities previously confined because of absence of full interaction" (1928a,
47–48)—and the most significant change is that *things*, in the widest
sense of the word, become meaningful, and that this meaning is a *shared*
meaning. Rather, therefore, than arguing that the material world is the
most fundamental world—which would be the materialistic reductionism
that can, for example, be found in certain forms of behaviorism—Dewey
suggested that the *social* world "is the widest and richest manifestation of

the whole accessible to our observation" (1928a, 53). The social is, in other words, the most complex and the most inclusive level of natural transaction and not a different ontological realm, a different realm of reality. There is therefore no need to tell a completely different story about inquiry into the social domain. If there is something special to say, it has to be an extension of the principles that are at stake in all inquiry.

From this it follows that there is also no fundamental difference in the way in which we should understand knowledge of the social domain. There is, in other words, no need to develop a special epistemology for social inquiry. Dewey simply took the position that "we know with respect to any subject-matter whatsoever in the degree in which we are able deliberately to transform doubtful situations in resolved ones" (1929a, 200). One important implication of this experimental approach to knowledge is that successful action is not the *result* of "true" knowledge, but rather its *precondition*. Dewey reminded us that modern physical science did not develop because inquirers piled up a mass of facts about observed phenomena, but because they intentionally experimented, on the basis of ideas and hypotheses, with observed phenomena to modify them and disclose new observations: "Men [*sic*] obtained knowledge of natural energies by trying deliberately to control the conditions of their operation. The result was knowledge, and then control on a larger scale by the application of what was learned" (1931, 66). It is for this reason that Dewey maintained that if we want to have something to which the name *social science* may be given, there is only one way to go about it, namely, "by entering the path of social planning and control" (1931, 67–68).

It should immediately be added, however, that when Dewey wrote about social planning and social control, he was not referring to a situation of top-down coercion where one person decides what another person should or should not do. For Dewey social planning and social control mean nothing more—and nothing less—than intelligent action in the social domain. (Recall what we said about Dewey's definition of "control" earlier.) Social planning and social control are, in other words, about the development of *social intelligence*. Dewey reminds us that all our action in the social domain is in a fundamental sense experimental. We always have the opportunity to act and respond on the basis of the best of our knowledge, but we can never be absolutely certain about what will follow from it. Furthermore, when we deliberately set out to change a situation, for example through the implementation of an educational policy, this is always, logically, of the nature of an experiment. This is not only because "it represents the adoption of one out of a number of alternative conceptions as possible plans of action," but also because "its execution is followed by consequences which . . . may serve as tests of the validity of the conception acted upon" (Dewey 1938a, 502).

All this amounts to saying that the differences between natural and social inquiry—or, as Dewey preferred to call it, the "study of man," the "inquiry into human relationships," or the "inquiry into cultures of associated life," since these labels do not prejudge the subject matter of study (1947, 224)—are only of a *gradual* nature. This is not to say, of course, that there are *no* relevant differences that should be taken into account when inquiring into human relationships. Two differences are of special significance here.

Inquiry into Human Relationships

First of all, a case can be made that the social domain is *more complex* than the natural domain. Part of the complexity has to do with the fact that it is more difficult to institute "a relatively closed system" (Dewey 1938a, 481) in the social domain. But again this difference is one of degree and not of kind, for one way of understanding the "success" of physical inquiry lies precisely in the fact that inquirers have been successful in separating out inquiry into the physical from its social context. This is one way to understand the difference between a "physical fact" and a "social fact," in that an occurrence can be called a physical fact "when its constituents and their relations remain the same, irrespective of the human attitude toward them" (Dewey 1931, 64). But Dewey hastened to add that this does not mean that physical facts exist independently of human concerns. The organization of physical inquiry in modern society is rather one in which the influence of cultural conditions has become *indirect* (Dewey 1938a, 481–82). Social tendencies and the problems attending them still evoke special emphasis on certain physical problems rather than on others. Against this background Dewey warned that the notion of the complete separation of science from the social environment "is a fallacy which encourages irresponsibility, on the part of scientists, regarding the social consequences of their work" (1938a, 483). The fact that the social domain appears to be more complex than the physical domain is, in other words, not the result of a fundamental difference between the subject matter of the two types of inquiry. It is only because it has been possible to reduce the complexity of the subject matter of physical inquiry by separating it out from the influences of the wider sociopolitical context. The difference is a construction and not a given. Of course this does not imply that we should expect something similar to happen in the field of social inquiry. The relative independence of inquiry in the physical domain was, after all, achieved by separating out the influences of the wider sociopolitical context. A similar move with respect to social inquiry is simply not possible for the very reason that social inquiry has to do with social problems, which, if separated from wider sociopolitical influences, would immediately cease to exist.

There is a further reason why the social domain not only appears to be more complex than the domain of physical inquiry but actually *is* more complex. Although Dewey maintained that the social world is continuous with the natural world, he did argue, as we have seen, that on the level of social interaction the physical is taken up into "a wider and more complex and delicate system of interactions" so that it takes on new properties. As we discussed in chapter 2, the crucial difference between the transaction of particles and the transaction of human beings lies in the fact that human beings do not react to the behavior of other human beings in the same way in which one particle causes another particle to move. Human beings instead respond to the *meaning* of the actions of their partners in interaction. The coordination of human action relies, in other words, on a continuous flow of predictions about the meaning of our partners' activities, a continuous flow of predictions about what our partners may want to achieve together with us. Coordination requires continuous anticipatory adjustments, and it is this that introduces another level of complexity to social interaction. To put it as simply as possible: While nature doesn't "think" about the possible ways in which it might respond to our actions, other human beings do not simply react, but react on the basis of their interpretation of our actions. Precisely here we find the nature of the special complexity of social interaction.

The second difference between the natural and the social world that needs to be taken into account in social inquiry has to do with what Dewey called the subjective nature of social facts. We have already alluded to this point, but we need to take it up once more to look at it from a slightly different angle. We have seen that Dewey called an occurrence a physical fact when its constituents and their relations remain the same, irrespective of the human attitude toward them. Physically speaking, he writes, a fact "is the ultimate residue after human purposes, desires, emotions, ideas and ideals have been systematically excluded" (1931, 64).

This implies that something is—or better, *becomes*—a social fact as a result of its inclusion into the network of human communication and purposeful interaction. Something becomes a social fact as a result of its "connection with any system of human purposes and consequences" (Dewey 1931, 65). Although, as we have seen, the difference between physical and social facts is a difference of degree, it is nonetheless significant for an appropriate understanding of the special character of social inquiry.

The Proper Task of Social Science

Some people would argue that to connect social facts with human desires, emotions, and ideals makes them subjective to an extent that renders it impossible to establish any "objective" or "scientific" conclusions. Dewey argued, however, that the greater evil would come from the situation where we would *not* see the connection between social facts and the subject matter of social inquiry more generally, on the one hand, and human purposes and consequences, on the other. This would lead to a situation in which social inquiry would only be allowed to deal with questions about *means*, questions about how to achieve certain ends and purposes, but *not* with questions about the ends and purposes of human (inter)action themselves. Such a situation would make social scientists into *technicians* who only approach problems as they are given to them and who keep within the framework in which social problems are presented to them (see Dewey 1947, 225). There is a real danger that this is what many, including politicians and policymakers, hope, expect, and sometimes even demand from social and educational research. Dewey provides strong arguments for resisting such simple expectations and demands.

In an essay with the significant title "Liberating the Social Scientist" (Dewey 1947, 224–38), Dewey forcefully argued against the idea that social scientists—those who conduct inquiries into human relationships and cultures of associated life—should occupy themselves exclusively with technical questions, that is, with questions about the ways in which pregiven ends can be achieved. His alternative, however, is not one of adding on a (moral) discussion about ends and purposes to the "proper" work of social science. Dewey rather argues that in *genuine* scientific inquiry the frame of reference is nothing more than a hypothesis, something that itself needs to be questioned and examined. It is precisely here that Dewey located the significance of twentieth-century developments in physical inquiry. Although since the sixteenth century physical inquiry has shown "an ever-growing respect for change," this respect was for a long time limited "by the Newtonian framework according to which change took place in changeless space and time" (Dewey 1947, 235). Dewey argued that it is the theory of relativity that has completed the tale, since it has made space and time into orders of events that are themselves susceptible to change (1951, 340).

For the conduct of social inquiry this first of all implies that we should never simply accept the problems as they present themselves. If we would do that, we would forget that what makes certain occurrences into social *problems* is precisely the fact that they are intimately connected with certain aims, ends, purposes, ideals, and aspirations. This is not to suggest that all social problems can simply be solved by changing the human context in which they occur. It is only to remind ourselves that when we simply take the problems as they are, we do not allow ourselves the opportunity for "analytic discrimination," which is one of the crucial activities in the transformation of an indeterminate situation into a problematic situation. This would lead to a situation in which the business of social inquiry would be restricted to finding the best method of solving the problems as they present themselves, rather than first trying to establish what the (social) problem actually *is*.

It also means that we should not assume that social facts are simply "out there" and only need to be "observed, assembled and arranged to give rise to suitable generalizations" (Dewey 1938a, 489). Once more, the point is that that social facts do not exist independently of human purpose, which means that they should at least be investigated on the basis of an adequate understanding of what constitutes these facts *as* social facts in the first place.

This finally brings us to the question of what Dewey's approach to social inquiry means in more practical terms. Although Dewey wanted to liberate the social scientist from the role of technician—that is, from the situation in which scientific inquiry is only allowed to say something about the most effective way to achieve certain ends—we have seen that he didn't want to give the social scientist an extra task. He rather argued that we should think of the proper task of scientific inquiry into the social domain as something that covers the whole spectrum of facts and values. It is not, therefore, to simply add judgments about ends to the process of inquiry, but rather to shift judgment in (social) inquiry to "means-ends" relationships. It is not only that we need to judge "existential materials" with respect to their function "as material means of effecting a resolved situation" (Dewey 1938a, 490). At the very same time and in one and the same process we need to evaluate ends "on the basis of the available means by which they can be attained" (Dewey 1938a, 490). In the transformation of an indeterminate situation into a determinate situation—which, as we have seen, is Dewey's way of describing intelligent problem solving—fixed and predetermined ends are useless (or at least pretty unhelpful). The point of the process of inquiry (and basically this holds for all inquiry) is to institute "means-consequences (ends) in *strict conjugate relation* to each other" (Dewey 1938a, 490). What we need in the process of inquiry, in other words, are what Dewey called "ends-in-view." Ends-in-view are hypotheses, which are essential for the proper conduct of inquiry. Dewey wrote, "Only an end-in-view that is treated as a *hypothesis* (by which discrimination and ordering of existential material is operatively effected) can by any logical possibility determine the existential materials that are means" (1938a, 490).

Dewey wrote, not without irony, that "[i]n all fields but the social" the notion that the correct solution is already given and that it only remains to find the facts that prove it, is so "thoroughly discredited" that those who act on it are regarded as pretenders or cranks (see Dewey 1938a, 490). It is only when we recognize that in both theory and practice, ends to be attained (ends-in-view) are of the nature of *hypotheses* and that these hypotheses have to be formed and tested "in strict correlativity with existential conditions as means" that a change in the "current habits of dealing with social issues" might be effected (see Dewey 1938a, 490). To become thoroughly pragmatist in social inquiry we need, in other words, to allow not only for an experimental approach toward means but also, and in strict conjugate relation to each other, for an experimental approach toward ends. It is only along these lines that social inquiry can help us find out not only whether what we desire is achievable, but also whether achieving it is desirable (we will return to this in chapter 5).

This discussion reveals that for Dewey intelligent action in the social domain is not about social engineering or social control in the narrow sense of these concepts. Action in the social domain can only become intelligent action when the subjective nature of social reality, that is, its intrinsic relationship with human purposes and consequences, is fully taken into account. From here it is only a small step to that form of social inquiry called "educational inquiry."

EDUCATIONAL INQUIRY

In a sense educational inquiry is indeed just one form of inquiry into human relations among many others. In this respect it does not pose any particular questions qua inquiry. The general pattern of inquiry is applicable to inquiry into the domain of education, just as the more specific issues that have to do with inquiry into human relationships.

Educational Practice

One thing that stands out in Dewey's discussion of educational inquiry is the central position of educational practice. Educational practice is "the beginning and the close" of all educational inquiry. On the one hand, it is the sole source of the problems to be investigated. It provides the data and the subject matter that form the problems of inquiry. On the other hand, educational practice is also "the final *test of value* of the conclusions of all researches" (Dewey 1929b, 16). Dewey explained,

> To suppose that scientific findings decide the value of educational undertakings is to reverse the real case. Actual activities in *educating* test the worth of scientific results. They may be scientific in some other field, but not in education until they serve educational purposes, and whether they really serve or not can be found out only in practice. (1929b, 26–27)

This is in line with Dewey's contention that education is an art and not a science—or, to be more precise: that it is an art that can be *informed* by science, that is, by the outcomes of educational inquiry.

Whereas educational practice occupies the central position in Dewey's understanding of educational inquiry, the educational practitioner is the central figure in the practice of education. Dewey emphasized again and again that the one and only purpose of educational inquiry is to make the actions of the educator more intelligent: "The sources of educational science," Dewey wrote, "are any portions of ascertained knowledge that enter into the heart, head and hands of educators, and which, by entering in, render the performance of the educational function more enlightened, more humane, more truly educational than it was before" (1929b, 39). Dewey even went as far as to say that the "final reality" of educational science is not found in books, laboratories, or classrooms, "but in the minds of those engaged in directing educational activities" (1929b, 16). This means that the outcomes of educational inquiry only become "educational science" when they are used, "through the medium of the minds of educators, to make educational functions more intelligent" (Dewey 1929b, 16). The outcomes of inquiry are sources of a science of education, but the point Dewey tried to make is that the actual "science of education" only exists in the use made of the outcomes of inquiry in the actual educational process.

It is against this background—and completely consistent with what we have seen so far—that Dewey emphasized that the conclusions of educational inquiry cannot be converted into immediate *rules* of educational action (1929b, 9). This is, obviously, not to suggest that educational inquiry is meaningless for the practice of education; Dewey believed quite the contrary. It is rather to highlight that the outcomes of previous inquiries do not specify successful lines of action for the future; they do not provide simple prescriptions of what should be done in the future. Educational inquiries provide "intellectual instrumentalities" (Dewey 1929b, 14) that can be used as "input" in new inquiries, that is, as resources for dealing with the always unique problems with which educators are faced. The results of previous inquiries can make educational action more intelligent, because they provide resources that enable educators to see new problems or see problems in a new light, to guide their observations, and to help them with interpreting the problematic situations they encounter. Dewey wrote,

> If we retain the world "rule" at all, we must say that scientific results furnish a rule for the conduct of *observations and inquiries*, not a rule for overt action. They function not directly with respect to practice and its results, but indirectly, through the medium of an altered mental attitude. (1929b, 15)

The results of educational inquiries provide educators with a wider range of alternatives from which to select, in dealing with individual situations. That is all they can do. They enrich the educator's ability to judge (see Dewey 1929b, 10). According to Dewey, this is the one and only way in which the results of educational inquiry can have an impact on educational practice.

The Educator as Investigator

One further implication of this view is that teachers should themselves be "investigators" (Dewey 1929b, 23). It is, after all, only when teachers approach their own educational practices in an experimental and investigative way, and not simply as a site for the application of educational laws and rules, that intelligent educational action becomes possible. In Dewey's own words, "[I]t is impossible to see how there can be an adequate flow of subject-matter to set and control the problems investigators deal with, unless there is active participation on the part of those directly engage in teaching" (1929b, 24). Dewey is arguing, therefore, that educational research should not simply be research on education and educators, but should involve educators themselves in a meaningful way.

All of this means that educational inquiry will never come to an end. In education we will constantly be faced with new, unique situations and new, unique problems. While on the one hand the outcomes of educational inquiry feed back into the educational process itself in order to render educational practice more intelligent, we will constantly find more problems to be further studied, "which then react into the educative process to change it still further, and thus demand more thought, more science, and so on, in everlasting sequence" (Dewey 1929b, 40). This means not only that we shouldn't expect firm solutions from educational inquiry, but that we can only hope for "instruments" that can help us in the never-ending process of dealing with educational problems. In a sense it also means that the idea of "improving" educational practice in any direct way through educational research should be abandoned—at least, that is, so long as we think of improvement as a process in which education becomes increasingly more perfect. Educational problems are always unique and for that reason always require unique responses, tailored as best as possible to the idiosyncrasies of the actual, unique situation. This, and nothing else, is what we should expect from educational inquiry.

Consequences of Pragmatism

To know is the characteristically human enterprise — a thing for men, not for gods or beasts.

—John Dewey (1911a, 68)

So far we have provided a reconstruction of Dewey's views on knowing and action in order to make clear what his ideas entail for educational inquiry and research. In the first chapter we presented the more general context of Dewey's philosophical project in order to make clear what Dewey wanted to achieve. The main purpose of this chapter is to look into the implications of Dewey's ideas. If, after all, Dewey's views would not be different in their consequences from other articulations of what knowing and knowledge are about, they would fail the very test that is at the center of pragmatist philosophy. In this chapter we therefore want to look at some of the consequences of Dewey's pragmatism in order to make clear where and how his ideas actually make a difference. We will focus on three issues that have not only been central to philosophical discussions about knowledge for many centuries, but that are also of crucial importance for any discussion about the point and purpose of educational research. We will first look at the implications of Dewey's views for our understanding of the relationship between theory and practice. Next we will discuss the question of the relationship between knowledge and reality. Finally we will address questions about objectivism and relativism from a Deweyan point of view. These three consequences of pragmatism don't only reveal what follows from taking a Deweyan perspective on knowledge and action. In chapter 1 we argued that the overall aim of Dewey's philosophy is to restore rationality, agency, and responsibility to the sphere of human action; in this chapter we will show that this is indeed the theme that unites the three issues under discussion.

THEORY AND PRACTICE

Dewey's ideas about knowing and its intimate relationship with action are not meant to establish a connection between the sphere of knowledge and the sphere of human action. It is not that he wants to restore the relationship between the world of matter and the world of mind, between the Cartesian *res extensa* and *res cogitans*. His aim, rather, is to "reintegrate human knowledge and action in the general framework of reality and natural processes" (Dewey 1939b, 80). The difference between the two approaches might be subtle but is decisive for an adequate understanding of Dewey's position. *The point is that Dewey was not looking for a way to connect or unite what is separate*. After all, he rejected the very assumption upon which modern philosophy has been erected, namely, that there is a gap between the sphere of knowing and the sphere of action—a gap, moreover, which is not merely of a methodological or epistemological nature, but is woven into the very fabric of the universe.

The End of Epistemology

As we briefly discussed in chapter 1, the dualistic framework of modern philosophy has had several problematic implications. It has first of all produced a distrust in our knowledge. Given the assumption that there is an unbridgeable gap between mind and matter, modern philosophy has argued that we can never be certain that our mind is "in touch" with reality. Modern philosophy thus has a built-in skepticism. Ever since the emergence of the modern dualistic worldview, philosophers have tried to give an answer to the question of how knowledge is possible. But this question—and the philosophical subdiscipline of epistemology that has been occupied with this question for many centuries—are themselves merely the product of the dualistic framework. As soon as this framework is put into question—and the point of Dewey's reconstruction of the history of modern philosophy is to show that this framework is the contingent outcome of the way in which modern thought has developed rather than the necessary point of departure for all philosophizing — we can move beyond the skepticism of modern philosophy and hence also beyond epistemology.

Dewey indeed declared the end of the "epistemological industry" (1917, 23; 1941, 179). He also argued that his philosophy is not "particularly skeptical" (1906a, 97). Dewey's rejection of the skepticism of modern philosophy does not mean, however, that he held that as soon as we see something we know it. Dewey maintained that all our knowledge is fallible, that "[a]ny one of our beliefs is subject to criticism, revision and even ultimate elimination through the development of its own implications by intelligently conducted action" (1906a, 98). But Dewey did not argue that all our knowledge is fallible because of an alledged gap between mind and reality, as a result of which we can never be sure that we are in touch with reality. It is simply because we can never be certain about what the future will bring:

> Agnosticism as confession of ignorance about special matters . . . is an act of intellectual honesty. But such skepticism and agnosticism are particular and depend upon special conditions; they are not wholesale; they do not issue from a generalized impeachment of the adequacy of the organs of knowing to perform their office (Dewey 1929a, 154).

Besides the fact that the dualistic framework of modern philosophy leads to the question of how we can know about the world in which we act, it also implies a separation between what we know and what we do. The question is, in other words, how our knowledge (which by the definition of modern philosophy is mental) can have an impact on our actions (which by definition belong to the material world). Dewey's transactionalism, as we have seen, does not situate knowledge outside the realm of action but thinks of it as a factor *in* organic action. Knowing is an activity, it is "a mode of doing" (see, e.g., 1916b, 367; 1929a, 184); it is the outcome of the cooperation of conceptual and existential operations. The knower, Dewey argued, is "within the world of existence; his knowing, as experimental, marks an interaction of one existence with other existences" (1929a, 236): "There is, however, a most important difference between it and other existential interactions. The difference is not between something going on within nature as a part of itself and something else taking place outside it, but is between a regulated course of changes and an uncontrolled one" (Dewey 1929a, 236). Knowledge, according to Dewey, is not only the *outcome* of the cooperation of conceptual and existential operations. His account of the process of inquiry reveals at the same time how knowledge—in the form of warranted assertions, in the form of possible connections between actions and consequences—feeds back into the process of experimental problem solving. It is along these lines that knowledge can have an impact on what we do.

One could of course object that along both lines Dewey made knowing an impossibility. If, after all, knowledge is something we do, that is, if it is an intervention in the state of affairs, reality will literally transform as a result of the very process of knowing so that we will never be able to grasp things as they really are. Dewey's reply here was that this is only a problem if we think of reality as a collection of ultimately static entities. Dewey's metaphysics of existence stipulates that reality itself has a practical character. This means that knowing is not the reduplication of reality, but the turning of reality "to account in behalf of consequences" (Dewey 1911a, 68). To think of knowledge as merely a reduplication in ideas of what exists already in the world may afford us "the satisfaction of a photograph," but that is all: "To form ideas whose worth is to be judged by what exists independently of them is not a function that (even if the test could be applied, which seems impossible) goes on within nature or makes any difference there" (Dewey 1929a, 110–11).

The Practice of Theory

If it is the case—and this, we have argued, is the central idea of Dewey's pragmatism—that knowing and acting are *necessarily* related, then it follows that one of the most important arguments for the (alleged) separation between theory as the domain where we acquire knowledge independent of our activities, and practice as the domain where we apply this knowledge, can no longer be sustained. According to Dewey there is, in other words, no epistemological difference, no epistemological separation, between the realm of theory and the realm of practice. This is not to suggest that it is impossible to make any distinction between theory and practice, but it is very important to be clear about what such a distinction entails and what it does not. Quite often we are inclined to refer, for example, to educational research or educational science as the realm of (educational) theory and to the actual work in schools or other educational settings as the realm of (educational) practice. And a brief look at the history of education shows that the question of the relationship between educational research and educational practice is one of the perennial questions of education (Condliffe-Lagemann 2000).

If we take a Deweyan perspective it becomes clear, however, that the difference between theory and practice is only a functional and gradual distinction. What we often refer to as theory and practice are, in fact, two different practices. It is not that the practice called "theory" only concerns itself with knowing while the practice called "practice" is only about action. Both practices contain a mix of knowing and action, the only possible difference being one of emphasis.

This conclusion also holds for one of the most prominent distinctions between theory and practice in the modern Western world, namely, the distinction between science and common sense. We have already seen that Dewey rejected the idea that science has a special method to access reality, a method different from the way in which we gain knowledge in our everyday lives. Dewey stressed that scientific inquiry "follows the same pattern as common sense inquiry" (1938a, 245). Dewey argued, in other words, that there is a *methodical continuity* between science and common sense. One of the most important implications of the principle of methodical continuity is that it becomes clear that any problems that have to do with or result from the relationship between science and common sense should not be understood as *epistemological* problems—they are thoroughly *social* problems that stem from the actual division of labor between science and common sense in society.

It has been asserted by several authors that in this argument Dewey simply put the traditional relationship between theory and practice on its head (Hickman 1990, 107). And to a certain extent this is correct. Dewey denounced the idea that theory is the highest thing that men can reach because it provides direct access to what is immutable and eternal, and hence true, while practice is inferior because it only deals with the world of action and contingency. Dewey gives priority to the practical and conceives of theory as a function of action. In this respect Dewey indeed seems to argue for a complete reversal of the traditional conception of the relationship between theory and practice. If, however, we follow Dewey in his claim that *theory* and *practice* are two different *practices*, then it seems more precise to say that Dewey denounced the idea that there is a *vertical* relationship between the two, in either direction, but rather that this relationship should be understood as a *horizontal* one.

Science and Common Sense

The foregoing ideas have important implications for the way in which we think about the role and position of science in society and, more specifically, for the way in which we conceive of the relationship between educational research and educational practice. In general terms we can say that the principle of methodical continuity does away with the idea that scientific knowledge—that is, knowledge produced by the social practice called "science"—should automatically possess cognitive authority, in other words, should be thought of as intrinsically better than our everyday knowledge. There could well be all kinds of different reasons for giving credence to the outcomes of scientific research, but these reasons are neither of an epistemological nature, nor are they categorically valid for all scientific research. They have to do with the specific conditions under which specific inquiries are conducted in specific settings. But the reason that *cannot* be given in order to give credence to the results of scientific research generally is that scientists are closer to reality "as it is" because they apply a special or more reliable method to gain their knowledge.

One of the implications of Dewey's account of the process of inquiry is that knowledge should never be understood as a statement of facts, but that knowledge always expresses *possibilities*—possibilities that in principle can be realized or become real. When we relate this to the principle of methodical continuity, the conclusion has to be that all knowledge is hypothetical with respect to concrete problematic situations. This further implies that the relationship between the results of scientific research and everyday practice is not a process in which the truths of science are simply handed down from the realm of science to the realm of practice and where the only thing that practice can do is to follow the discoveries of science. The Deweyan approach implies that science produces possibilites that can be used by practitioners in their day-to-day actions—and more specifically in their own inquiries, their own attempts to address the problems that confront them.

Along these lines Dewey opened up a new way of thinking about the relationship between theory and practice, between science and common sense, and hence between educational research and educational practice. Dewey presented knowledge—scientific knowledge, knowledge that has been produced by educational research(ers)—as an *instrument* that can help us to find out what the meaning of our immediate (problematic) experience is or might be, so that there is a better chance to find a way to restore coordinated action, a way, in short, to solve the problems we are faced with. The teacher with the disruptive student, an example from chapter 3, may find research useful and relevant to how she understands and copes with her problematic situation, but not as a recipe that can tell her directly what to do.

On Dewey's view, knowledge and theory more generally are very practical instruments. He wrote, "The paradox of theory and practice is that theory is with respect to all other modes of practice the most practical of all things, and the more impartial and impersonal it is, the more truly practical it is. And this is the sole paradox" (1915b, 82). The Deweyan way of thinking about the relationship between science and common sense and, more specifically, the relationship between (educational) research and (educational) practice may help us to restore the balance between the two areas, a balance that has been distorted as a result of the assumption that science presents us with a special kind of knowledge. From the point of view of common sense the Deweyan approach might help create a situation in which it is no longer assumed that scientific claims are intrinsically and automatically better or of more worth. From the point of view of science the Deweyan approach might help to be more modest—and more realistic—about what science can achieve and what it cannot. While in many cases there is still a long way to go, Dewey's approach at least opens up the possibility for a different, less authoritarian and more democratic approch to the relationship between theory and practice, science and society, educational research and educational practice.

It could be argued, however, that although the situation could be improved and problems might be solved if we all would adopt a Deweyan perspective on knowing and coming to know, there is a deeper problem that needs to be addressed. In many cases—not only those involving the natural sciences—the problem is not so much a matter of reconciling different possible stories to tell about experience; it is a matter of reconciling different accounts of what reality is *really* like. Even if we opt for a change in our conception of knowledge, the more difficult problem of different claims about reality—the scientific worldview versus the worldview of our everyday experience—would still remain. The reconciliation would, in other words, only be psychological. Dewey explicitly rejected such a psychological reading of his "instrumentalist" conception of knowledge when he wrote, "[M]any critics take an 'instrumental' theory of knowledge to signify that the value of knowing is instrumental to the knower. . . . But 'instrumentalism' is a theory not about

personal disposition and satisfaction in knowing" (1925a, 121). In order
to understand what Dewey's instrumentalism is all about, and in order to
be able to address in a more profound way the tension between the world
presented by scientific research and the world of our everyday experience,
we need to shift to the second topic of this chapter, which has to do with
the realism of Dewey's pragmatism.

THE REALISM OF PRAGMATISM

There are two issues that need to be taken into consideration when
discussing Dewey's ideas about the relationship between knowledge and
reality. The first is the general question about the "reality" of knowledge.
The second is the more specific question of how we should conceive of
the relationship between the world of everyday experience and the world
of scientific research.

The Reality of Knowledge

Dewey stressed many times that the presuppositions and tendencies of his
pragmatism are distinctly realistic. His pragmatism is not an idealism in
which everything only exists "in the mind" or where knowledge is nothing
but a mental construction. We are in touch with a real world, and our
knowledge is related to this reality as well. Although we can therefore
qualify Dewey's philosophy as expressing a version of realism and *not* of
idealism, Dewey's realism differs from other versions of realism in at least
two ways. First of all, Dewey rejected the idea that the only conceivable
way to think of reality is as a collection of macroscopic or microscopic
material entities. Dewey's metaphysics of existence specifies reality as
process and not as material-entities-in-process. Second, Dewey
denounced the idea that the only conceivable way to speak about reality
would be in terms of a reality completely independent from human
beings. Dewey stressed again and again that we are not spectators to a
finished universe but participants in an ever-evolving universe. If we want
to say anything about "reality," we will therefore always have to account
for our own presence in it. This is why, following Sleeper (1986, 92), we
have described Dewey's realism as *transactional realism*.

  In the previous chapters we discussed how in Dewey's transactional
realism knowledge relates to reality. The relationship between knowledge

and reality is not one of a static correspondence. If we want to use the idea of correspondence it must be in a temporal-transactional sense, that is, as a correspondence in time between "purpose, plan, and its own execution, fulfilment" (Dewey 1907a, 84). The correspondence is, in other words, a *functional* correspondence that is achieved when our conceptual operations are able to suggest activities through which a predicted change can be effected. It is because action—or more specifically the transaction of organism and environment—is involved that the warranted assertions following from the process of inquiry relate to reality.

Dewey's temporal-transactional understanding of the process of knowing and coming to know implies that knowledge is not the agreement between our ideas of reality and how reality "as such" is, but that knowledge is always *knowledge-of-relations*. This becomes especially visible in the method of modern natural science—which, as we have seen in the previous section, is not a special method but only "an intensified form of knowing in which are written large the essential characters of any knowing" (Dewey 1929a, 200). According to Dewey, the method of physical inquiry "is to introduce some change in order to see what other change ensues" (1929a, 68). The point of this method is to find "constant relations among changes" (Dewey 1929a, 82) or "the correlation between changes" (Dewey 1929a, 68). This clearly reveals the importance of existential operations in the process of knowing, either as the manipulation of or intervention into what is being investigated, or as the changing of the conditions under which what is being investigated is observed and examined.

It is important to note here that Dewey did not describe the essence of the scientific method as one in which we introduce change in order to see how the object or situation in which we introduce these changes itself changes. After all, that would put us again in the very spectator position that Dewey wanted to overcome. To appreciate the difference Dewey wanted to make, we need to take a closer look at what he, at one stage in has career, called his "radical empiricism" (1905, 158).

The central claim of Dewey's radical empiricism is that our perceptions "are the sole ultimate data, the sole media, of inference to all natural objects and processes" (1911c, 109). While we do not *know* our perceptions in any intelligible or verifiable sense, but only simply *have* them, Dewey's approach entails that we do know all that we know "*with* or *by* them" (1911c, 109). The central role, here, is for the "doings," our actions and activities. It is, after all, because our perceptions are inserted in the undergoing-doing-undergoing sequence that it becomes possible to establish what our perceptions might mean. When Dewey defined knowledge in terms of the correlation between changes, he was, therefore, not talking about changes that take place in the world outside, but about the correlation between our perceptions at moment t_1, our activities at moment t_2, and our perceptions at moment t_3.

Although Dewey was clear about what his position entails and what it does not, it seems that his radical empiricism is quite at odds with both the realism of our everyday lives and the realism of the (natural) sciences. The world of everyday experience is preeminently a world of objects, and in our everyday interaction with these objects we seem to know very well what these objects are. Albeit on a different scale, the same can be said about the world in which scientists work. Again, everything seems to suggest that the very point of scientists' activities is to find out as much as possible about all the (micro) objects that populate the world of nature, and although it seems plausible to argue, therefore, that we live our everyday and scientific lives in a world of objects, it might well be that this naive realism puts us on the wrong track, philosophically speaking. This is precisely the point Dewey made when he argued that if anything is in need of philosophical explanation it is not our *perception* of objects, but our perception of *objects*, that is, the fact that our perception is not blurred and vague but that we see clear-cut objects full of meaning (Dewey 1930c, 253). We see tables, chairs, cars, trees, other human beings; the trained eye of a doctor can immediately see a disease; the trained ear of a musician can immediately hear chords, and so on. What, then, is the status of the objects of our perception and the objects of our knowledge? And how real are they, according to Dewey's pragmatism?

The Objects of Knowledge

Dewey's transactionalism implies that the objects of everyday experience are to be understood as emerging from the transaction of human beings with their environment. We can think of these objects as the structure or form that the transaction takes over time. This is not some kind of mysterious process occurring out of the reach of human beings; it is, rather, the result of the way in which the transaction develops over time. In this respect the transformation of the transaction is real. As we briefly discussed in chapter 2, the structuring of the transaction of the human organism and its environment is effected by habits. In terms of visual perception Dewey explained that the perception of objects should be understood as "an ordering and organizing of responses in a single focussed way in virtue of which the original blur is definitized and rendered significant" (1929a, 190). Habits are crucial in this process, since without habits dealing with "the recurrent and constant uses of things for abiding purposes," immediate perception "would never have either rich nor clear meaning immanent within it" (Dewey 1929a, 190). The objects of perception are, therefore, located in the transaction of organism and environment. They are the form that this *transaction* takes, and not the form that reality "as such" takes.

Since knowing is only one mode of experience, Dewey stressed that the objects of everyday experience, the objects of common sense, cover the whole range of human qualities. Commonsense experience is of objects "which are colored, sonorous, tactile, gustatory, loved, hated, enjoyed, admired, which are attractive and repulsive, exciting, indifferent and depressive" (Dewey 1925a, 114). The question of knowledge has to do with the ways in which the objects of our immediate perception can serve as signs that, through our actions and activities, can result in other experiences. This, as we have seen before, implies that knowledge is concerned with the relationship between experienced objects, and not with the objects as such. It further implies that in the case of knowing we must to a certain extent distance ourselves from the meanings the objects of everyday experience have for us. Knowledge takes its point of departure in the objects of our everyday experience and, as we will show, eventually returns to these objects, but it doesn't coincide with the objects.

This means that the objects of everyday experience cannot be understood as objects of knowledge, in other words, as objects about which knowledge should be acquired. It may seem as if the process of coming to know is about getting to know more and more about the objects of our everyday experience, but this, so Dewey argued, is putting the cart before the horse. The object of knowledge is not something that has being prior to and independent of the operations of knowing. It is, as Dewey put it, *eventual*, that is, "it is an outcome of directed experimental operations, instead of something in sufficient existence before the act of knowing" (1929a, 136–37). The object of knowledge, then, emerges from experimental transactions with our environment. It is crucial for understanding this point to see the distinction between, for example, *this* table as it is immediately experienced, and *the* table as an object of knowledge. People can have all kinds of different experiences, such as a beautiful table, an ugly table, a table to which one is attached because it has been in the family for a long time, a red table, a table that blocks the way, et cetera. These are all different immediate experiences; they are experiences of different *this-es*. "'This,'" Dewey wrote, "undergoes change all the time," not in the least because from a transactional point of view *we* change all the time (1929a, 189).

Although there is an infinite range of different immediate experiences, it is, for example, possible to follow the *experience* of a red table or a table to which one has become attached (an experience that is in some sense personal or idiosyncratic) with an *activity* such as putting something on the table, which then is followed by the *experience* that what is put on the table stays there (an experience that may be shared by others). Hence, starting from different immediate experiences, different "things," different qualitative experiences, we can, through the intervention of action, end up with similar immediate experiences. We can, in other words, discover a constant among the multitude of relations. This constant, according to Dewey, is the *object of knowledge*. "*The* table," he explains, "is precisely the constancy among the serial 'thises' of whatever serves for a single end" (1929a, 189).

The table, as an object of knowledge, should therefore be understood as an *instrument* or a *tool*. It is, after all, by recognizing *this* table as *a* table that our qualitative experience of this table can be connected to several possible consequences, which are not simply there in the experienced "this-ness," the qualitative experience of *this* table. Such connections can help us to find an appropriate response to *this* table. Or, viewed from a different perspective: By constructing *a* table out of the infinite number of different tables, the transaction with the environment becomes more structured; it is no longer that we shift from one unique immediate experience to the next—we start to recognize pattern, structure, and form.

Dewey's Instrumentalism

The foregoing makes clear that the objects of knowledge—as distinct from the objects of our immediate qualitative experience—are not simply there to be experienced. They are *constructed*. Dewey explicitly states that we should think of the object of knowledge as a construction (1929a, 168). But Dewey's constructivism must, of course, be understood transactionally. The object of knowledge is constructed out of, as a result of, as a function of, the transaction: "Any instrument which is to operate effectively in existence must take account of what exists. . . . But 'taking account of' . . . is something quite different from literal conformity to what is already in being" (Dewey 1929a, 165). This also means that we do not construct the objects of knowledge out of the blue. They are not fantasies, things made up only in our minds. Just as we can only make effective instruments out of raw materials, the objects of knowledge have to be constructed out of available "materials."

Just as the objects of our everyday knowledge are constructed, Dewey argued that the objects of scientific inquiry are constructed as well. There is, after all, no fundamental difference between scientific and everyday inquiry. If there is a difference, it has to be a *practical* difference. Dewey suggested that the main practical difference between the objects that we construct in our everyday life and the objects constructed in scientific inquiry lies in the range of possible uses of the respective objects. The table corresponds to a limited number of possible uses. But if we think of the table as consisting of molecules, the range of possible uses or possible responses increases dramatically: "[T]he physical object . . . enables things qualitatively unlike and individual to be treated as if they were members of a comprehensive, homogeneous, or non-qualitative system. The possibility of control of the *occurrence* of individualized objects is thereby increased" (Dewey 1929a, 192). This, so Dewey argued, is the only difference between the objects of knowledge of our everyday life and the objects of knowledge constructed by science. The objects of science are not more real (or "fundamental" or "true") than the objects of our everyday experience—nor are they less real (that is, "theoretical" or "abstract"). They all emerge from the transaction with our environment and only differ because they serve different purposes. But there is no logical or epistemological gulf between the two kinds of objects. The only possible difference lies in the range of possible relations between experience and action in that the objects of science generally allow for a larger range of possible connections than the objects of our everyday knowledge. But in both cases the immediate qualitative experience is both the point of departure and the point of termination. "The final thing," Dewey wrote, "is appreciation and use of things of direct experience" (1929a, 177). This implies that besides the methical continuity between science and common sense there is also a continuity in terms of content. Science doesn't have its own access to reality; it always has to go back to the immediate qualitative experience as well.

Theory and Practice, Science and Common Sense

Dewey's transactional realism and the implications of this view for our understanding of the status of our objects of knowledge and, subsequently, the status of the objects of our immediate, qualitative experience, suggest a way out of the problem that emerged at the end of the previous section, which was how to reconcile the reality of our everyday experience with the reality of modern science. Dewey's instrumentalism not only shows that the objects of knowledge constructed by science do not differ fundamentally from the objects of knowledge constructed in our day-to-day transactions. It also shows the connection between objects of knowledge and our immediate, qualitative experience. What follows from this is that the world of science is not a competitor to the world of common sense. Both the objects of knowledge of science and of common sense are, as Dewey put it, a means "for securing and avoiding immediate objects" (Dewey 1925a, 114). The conclusion, therefore, is that the objects of natural science are not metaphysical rivals of the objects of our immediate qualitative experience; they are "means of directing the latter" (Dewey 1925a, 119). In Dewey's own words,

> What science actually does is to show that any natural objects we please may be treated in terms of relations upon which its occurrence depends, or as an event, and that by so treating it we are enabled to get behind, as it were, the immediate qualities the object of direct experience presents, and to regulate their happening, instead of having to wait for conditions beyond our control to bring it about. (1929a, 84)

This, once more, reveals that the central theme of Dewey's investigations was to make clear that knowledge plays a role in and for action, rather than that action should simply follow what knowledge dictates. In the case of the relationship between scientific research and human practices, we can again say that the point of research should be to help and support what takes place in human practices, not in order to say what should or should not happen, but rather to enable those who engage in human practices—including the practice of education—to achieve what they want or think should be achieved.

Dewey's instrumentalism, which builds on his transactional realism, makes it possible to solve the alleged problem of the competition between the reality of science and the reality of everyday life. Rather than thinking of this as a competition between two realities where the final verdict has to be one in terms of which reality is "more real," Dewey shows that the reality of science and the reality of everyday life, insofar as both realities are made up of objects of knowledge, are simply two collections of instruments. Dewey showed that there is no point in asking about the degree of reality—or, as we have seen, even the truth—of instruments. The only meaningful question has to do with what we can use these instruments for. If we think of all the objects of knowledge produced in all kinds of different contexts—scientific and otherwise—as possible instruments for our everyday action, the question will no longer be one of which instrument should have priority (because it would be more real), but rather how the different instruments, the different objects of knowledge, can cooperate in the most helpful way in order to address the problems we are faced with in our everyday lives. From a theoretical question about the reconciliation of the world of science and the world of common sense, we then move to the *practical* question about the integration, cooperation, and coordination of the different instruments available to us. Certainly one implication of this view is that there is no reason to prioritize the knowledge produced by professional educational researchers over the knowledge produced by teachers reflecting upon and learning from their own experiences—but by the same token, there would be no reason to automatically prioritize them the other way around, either. Both sorts of errors are rampant in educational thought, and Dewey provides us with a way to avoid them.

BEYOND OBJECTIVISM AND RELATIVISM

The third and final implication of Dewey's pragmatism stems from the question of whether Dewey's views on knowledge and coming to know allow us to discriminate between valid and invalid knowledge, valid and invalid belief, or whether it is the case, as many critics have argued, that Dewey's views imply subjectivism and relativism.

The Subjectivity of Knowledge

Central to Dewey's understanding of knowledge and coming to know is the concern for bringing about desirable situations. As we have seen, this is not just what drives the process of inquiry. More generally, the point of knowledge is not to know more simply for the sake of knowing, but to be able to exert greater control over the problematic situations we find ourselves in. The purpose of knowing seems, therefore, to be very closely connected to individual satisfaction. It is for this reason that Dewey has frequently been accused of subjectivism.

Critics—such as Bertrand Russell (1940, chapter 23)—argued that Dewey's pragmatism identifies truth with, and hence reduces truth to, individual satisfaction. This argument seems to accuse pragmatism of holding that whatever pleases us or provides satisfaction to us is true. Although Dewey often refers to "doubt" or "uncertainty" as that which instigates a process of inquiry, and the removal of doubt or uncertainty as the outcome of successful inquiry, he does not mean that doubt and uncertainty only exist on the side of the individual—they are, rather, characteristics of the transaction. For this reason solving the problem, or restoring coordination, is not possible by simply satisfying the individual. What is needed is a transformation of all constitutive elements of the transaction. Although it is true that the *perception* of the indeterminateness of the situation is something located on the side of the individual, and in that respect can be called mental or subjective, this does not imply that the indeterminateness of the situation is itself mental or subjective. Dewey argued that "irrespective of whether a satisfaction is conscious, a satisfaction or non-satisfaction is an objective thing with objective conditions. It means fulfillment of the demands of objective factors" (1925a, 59). As long as one keeps the transactional framework of Dewey's philosophy in mind—and unfortunately many critics of Dewey forget to do this—there is no reason whatsoever for accusing Dewey of subjectivism.

There is, however, a different line of critique that seems to be more to the point and that leads to a slightly more complex discussion. As we have seen, Dewey argued that the object of knowledge is the *outcome* of the processes of inquiry. The "true object of knowledge," he argued, "resides in the consequences of directed action" (1929a, 157). This view implies, however, that there will be as many kinds of known objects as there are kinds of effectively conducted operations of inquiry that result in the consequences intended. It further implies that there are as many kinds of valid knowledge as there are conclusions wherein distinctive operations have been employed to solve the problems set by antecedently experienced situations (Dewey 1929a, 157). The upshot of these views seems to be that every individual creates his or her own world and, hence, his or her own truths. Since this implies that there are many different subjective worlds and truths, and no objective one, this seems to imply a situation of not only complete subjectivism, but a total relativism, since ultimately, everyone has his or her own truth.

We might agree that in this respect Dewey's pragmatism indeed does lead to subjectivism, but not necessarily a pernicious one. Dewey acknowledged that each individual, in his or her unique transaction with his or her environment, informed by his or her unique past experiences, does create his or her own individual and idiosyncratic world. In one sense this is true by definition. But he hastens to add that this is not a problem. After all, these are wholly private matters and "[b]eing nobody else's business, it is absurd to regard them as either true or false" (Dewey 1911a, 19). Questions about truth and falsity, questions about how to represent our individual objects of knowledge and our immediate experiences, only become relevant in social situations—situations in which we act together with others. Dewey explains, "To represent things as they are is to represent them in ways that tend to maintain a common understanding . . . and understanding is a social necessity because it is a prerequisite of all community of action" (1911a, 16). It is only in and as a result of social interaction that the need arises to coordinate our individual, idiosyncratic worlds in order to bring about a sufficient degree of common understanding—where, in Dewey's action theoretical framework, common understanding is not primarily mental but first of all a "likeness of attitude" or "agreement as to proper diversity of attitude" (Dewey 1911a, 17). It is in this way that we create a common, an "intersubjective," world. For Dewey truth and truthful representation are not issues that arise in our individual transaction with the environment. It is not, therefore, "the object alone which decides what is the proper and authorized account of itself; but the object as a term and factor in established social practice" (1911a, 19–20). Dewey even takes this one step further by arguing that truth is first of all a *social* virtue, meeting a demand growing out of social intercourse, and not a logical, much less an epistemological, relation. He therefore suggests that the opposite of truth is not *error* but *lying* (Dewey 1911a, 14–15).

The Relativity of Knowledge

We believe that the foregoing argument provides an adequate answer to the accusation of subjectivism. Dewey clearly showed where and when his philosophy indeed is subjectivistic, and he provided arguments for making clear why this should not worry us. He also made it perfectly clear when questions about the truth and falsity of our knowledge, about the validity of our beliefs, *do* make sense and even when they become urgent—which is in the situation of social interaction. Hence it is important to notice that Dewey's alternative for subjectivism is not objectivism, that is, a situation in which we should represent the objects of our knowledge in some way that is independent of any human concern. For Dewey this would not be possible. His alternative for subjectivism is called *inter*subjectivity. We first construct our objects of knowledge on a strictly individual level and in a strictly individual and idiosyncratic way, but then co-construct—or better, co-reconstruct—these objects by introducing them into our social practices.

One of the implications of this view is that it is impossible to make a hard distinction between "traits belonging to the thing as thing" and "traits belonging in virtue of social custom" (Dewey 1911a, 20). Besides the primary qualities of objects, such as solidity, extension, and shape, and secondary qualities of objects, such as sounds, tastes, colors, and smells (a distinction made by John Locke), and besides so-called tertiary qualities such as pleasantness, sadness, feebleness, splendidness, or wickedness (a notion introduced by the American philosopher George Santayana), Dewey suggested that we may also speak of quaternary qualities: "the qualities that custom prescribes as properly belonging to objects in virtue of their being factors in a social life" (1911a, 21).

Although Dewey seems to be able to ward off the accusation of subjectivism, it does seem to lead him directly into a kind of relativism. If it is the case that the representation of things in accordance with their own nature actually comes down to a representation according to the requirements of social tradition, this seems to imply that knowledge becomes dependent on and hence "relative to" that tradition. Many people would argue that relativism in this sense is a problem because it renders it impossible to make any definitive, context- or tradition-independent decision about which knowledge claims should be adhered to and which not. Are the critics right, therefore, that if we follow Dewey's pragmatism, anything goes?

Part of Dewey's answer lies, as we have already seen, in his transactionalism, which clearly limits what it is possible to accept as "true." But there is another line of argument in Dewey's writings that we need to explore in order to get a full understanding of the way in which his pragmatism deals with questions about the relativity of knowledge.

The point to begin with is to acknowledge that although Dewey stressed that social custom and tradition are part of our knowledge and that there is no way in which they can be expunged, he does see severe problems in making knowledge totally dependent upon tradition and custom. The most important of these problems is that in such a situation we would not have an opportunity to be critical of tradition and custom themselves.

As long as there is no reason to question custom and tradition, there is of course no problem. But as soon as we want to question the status quo, we cannot rely on the status quo itself to provide us with the means for doing so. Dewey suggested that Western philosophy was born at the very moment when custom could no longer maintain itself as a final standard of life. Plato suggested a shift from the life of tradition as the ultimate standard, to a reality *beyond* tradition (see Dewey 1911a, 26). We have already seen, however, that Dewey finds this shift problematic because it makes truth and knowledge into something disconnected from human life, disconnected from any real human concern. He writes, "If there be truth eternal and absolute, and yet that truth cannot become operative in human affairs so as to extend and secure their prosperity, the existence and nature of absolute truth may be of interest to discarnate angelic beings, but not to man [*sic*] as human" (1911a, 54).

One important component of Dewey's answer here is to be found in his *consequentialism*. He observes that the Platonic shift from tradition to transcendental reality is only a shift from one absolute foundation to another. The point of Dewey's pragmatism is *not* simply to stipulate a different foundation. Pragmatism does not look back (to tradition and custom) in order to find the foundation for our knowledge; it suggests that we look forward, that is, that we focus on the consequences of our actions and ideas. For pragmatism the crucial question always has to do with what might follow when we act in a specific way or follow some idea. Knowledge itself, as we have seen, is nothing but an articulation of the possible connection between what we do and what will follow. Our objects of knowledge can also be understood as summarizing possible relations between doing and undergoing. And *truth*—to the extent to which this word has a meaning in Dewey's vocabulary at all—is eventually concerned with working toward the concrete production of specific consequences as well.

In this respect Dewey's pragmatism clearly differs from the foundationalist strategies of both traditionalism and Platonism. The critical question that remains to be answered is, however, *what kind of consequences* should be taken into consideration? Should we eventually give primacy to purely intellectual consequences, or should we emphasize the social consequences? It will not come as a surprise that Dewey did not want us to make a choice for either of these options, but wanted us to look for a way to integrate both perspectives: "My hypothesis is that the standpoint and method of science do not mean the abandonment of social purpose and welfare as rightfully governing criteria in the formation of beliefs, but that they signalize a profound transformation in the nature of social purpose and social welfare" (1911a 57). Dewey's elaboration of this hypothesis consisted of two steps. First he argued that the intellectual or scientific perspective does not necessarily exclude the social perspective. The values that characterize the intellectual perspective—such as impartiality, impersonality, and value freedom—are only in opposition to fixed or preestablished values, but not to values as such. What the intellectual perspective excludes, in other words, is *dogmatism*: "To be intellectually objective," Dewey wrote, "is to be impartial; to have no ax to grind; no preconceived purpose to maintain at any cost; no particular consequence to insist upon at any hazard" (1911a, 60). If we would always already know beforehand what would be valuable or desirable and what not, consequentialism would be seriously hampered. It would lead to a situation in which the social would restrict the intellectual.

This does not mean, however, that the intellectual or scientific perspective should be allowed to decide what should happen and what should not, what is desirable and what is not. This would result in the positivism that, as we showed in chapter 1, Dewey wanted to overcome. The intellectual or scientific perspective can help us to establish what is— or what might be—possible. It can provide us with means to achieve our ends. Dewey argued, however, that progress "is not adequately conceived when we regard it as merely a greater command of the means for realizing ends with which we are already familiar" (1911a, 60). The integration of the intellectual and social perspective that Dewey tried to achieve is one in which we become more "scientific"—that is, experimentalistic and consequentialistic—about our aims and objectives: "Significant progress, progress which is more than technical, depends upon the ability to foresee new and different results and to arrange conditions for their effectuation" (1915b, 81). This is, of course, not something that scientists can do for us. The deliberation about aims and ends, about what is desirable and what is not, should be a *public* deliberation. It is precisely here that the value of democracy becomes central and inextricably connected to our considerations about knowing and coming to know. If the worth of intersubjective knowledge depends on the traditions and practices of the community in which they are formed, then the capacities for deliberation about and testing of those claims become a central measure of the worth of that community—and indeed for Dewey this is the chief advantage of democratic systems.

It is further important to notice that a public, democratic deliberation about ends should not be thought of as disconnected from a deliberation about means. It is not that we simply can decide what we want to achieve and then try to find the best means for achieving it. While *initially* we may think that a certain end is desirable, it is only when we know what it would cost us to achieve that end—that is, when we know *how* to achieve it— that we can decide whether what we wanted to achieve is really desirable. It may well be that once we know how we can achieve what we want to achieve, we must come to the conclusion that the price—literally, or ethically, or socially, or for environmental reasons—is simply too high or even unacceptable. We only know, in other words, what an aim entails once we know how we can achieve it. Here we see the import of Dewey's argument that the intellectual or scientific perspective should inform our deliberation about aims and ends, about what is desirable and what is not, and that this weighing of aims and ends must have a social, intersubjective dimension.

From Relativism to Humanism

The foregoing section clearly reveals that for Dewey the social is an inextricable part of our knowledge and the process of coming to know. It also makes clear, however, that Dewey was not advocating a flat-out relativism in which the intellectual becomes totally dependent on the social. Dewey opts for an integration of the social and the intellectual perspective. This integration works in two directions. On the one hand, he argues for an experiential approach with regards to our aims and values. We need to deliberate about what we want to achieve, and we should do so in a systematic, experimental, and democratic way in order to overcome stifling dogmatism. Not only do we need input from the intellectual perspective (science), in order to find out whether what we want to achieve is possible and, if so, at what price. Dewey also suggested that the methods of inquiry provide a systematic way of experimenting with and deliberating about aims and values. Along these lines the intellectual should transform the social.

On the other hand, Dewey stressed again and again that the intellectual on its own, without a clear social context and setting, is meaningless: first and foremost because to know is a characteristically human enterprise—"a thing for men [*sic*], not for gods or beasts" (1911a, 68). In this respect truth can only be *human* truth, in other words, an interpretation of things "that make[s] these things effectively function in liberation of human purpose and efficiency of human effort" (Dewey 1911a, 66). This implies, as we have seen in the previous chapter, that verification is not something that takes place solely within the confines of the scientific laboratory or its equivalent, but something that needs the widest application possible.

Is this relativism? In a sense we have agreed that it is, because Dewey rejected the idea that it is possible (or meaningful) to think of knowledge outside of and totally disconnected from any human concern. As he put it, "Truth, in final analysis, is a statement of things 'as they are,' not as they are in the inane and desolate void of isolation from human concern, but as they are in a shared and progressive experience" (1911a, 67). But this does not mean that anything is possible, or that individual satisfaction would be the only relevant criterion for truth: "[W]hat the pragmatist does is to insist that the human factor must work itself out in *cooperation* with the environmental factor, and that their coadaptation *is* both 'correspondence' and 'satisfaction'" (Dewey 1910, 10).

Dewey refused to put all his eggs in the intellectual basket. One very practical reason for this is that if we would forget or deny the human factor, this factor will manifest itself anyhow, but in an unexpected, uncontrollable and eventually irresponsible way (Dewey 1910, 10). In this respect "inhuman rationality" is not only undesirable but dangerous.

Nothing said here prevents one from calling Dewey's position "relativistic." But it does raise the question of whether and to what extent this label is any longer meaningful in the context of Dewey's pragmatism. His argument that knowledge is neither objective nor subjective, but is thoroughly *inter*subjective, suggests that he goes beyond the framework from which the very distinction between objectivism and relativism gets its meaning. It is for this reason that Dewey suggested to refer to his position not as relativism but as *humanism* (Dewey 1911a, 65).

CONCLUSION

In this chapter we have presented three interrelated consequences of Dewey's pragmatism: his ideas about the relationship between theory and practice, his ideas about the reality of knowledge, and his views on objectivism and relativism. In all three cases Dewey had something new and interesting to offer.

Dewey's action-theoretical framework does away with the idea that there is an epistemological difference between theory and practice. It is not that theory can tell us how things are and that practice merely has to follow. If, as Dewey argued, knowledge is indeed a factor *in* human action, then theory no longer comes before practice, but emerges from and feeds back into practice. If, therefore, we would want to make a distinction between theory and practice—for example in the case of educational research and educational practice, or in the case of science and common sense more generally—we are not making an epistemological distinction, but a thoroughly social one. Science—including educational science and educational research—is as much a practice as (educational) practice is. This does not make science and practice identical, but it does away with the idea that the difference between the two practices is an epistemological difference, one in which science is purely concerned with knowledge and practice is purely concerned with action.

As soon as this link is acknowledged, we can begin to ask different questions about the relationship between science and common sense, between educational research and educational practice. On the one hand, it becomes much more important to ask empirical and historical questions about the actual (power) relationships between science and common sense and between educational research and educational practice. On the other hand, Dewey's perspective invites us to think in different ways about how the relationship between theory and practice should be drawn. In this respect Dewey's suggestion that the knowledge produced by science is not simply a truth to follow but a *possibility* that we can use in our everyday problem solving has a lot to offer a field like education. Along both lines Dewey's approach shows that science is a more human and down-to-earth enterprise than the epistemological interpretation allows us to recognize. His rejection of the idea that practice should simply follow theory also implies a recognition of the reflective potential that is present in many practices.

The second consequence of Dewey's pragmatism—his ideas about the way in which our knowledge relates to reality—can, in a sense, be seen as further support for his views about theory and practice. The main point is that the world of science and the world of common sense should not be understood as two competing worlds, and definitely not as two worlds competing about which world is closer to some "real" reality. Dewey's transactional realism implies that we construct our objects of knowledge in order to inform and support our actions. Our objects of knowledge are instruments, and the only meaningful question to ask about them is which instruments are most appropriate in dealing with the problems that we encounter in our lives. There is, therefore, no theoretical question about how we can reconcile the "truths" of science with the "truths" of our everyday life. There are only practical questions about how we can use the different instruments that are available to us in an effective and responsible way.

The third consequence of Dewey's pragmatism—his answer to allegations of subjectivism and relativism—reveals once more that the point of his pragmatism is not to play knowledge and science against human concerns, but to find meaningful ways of integration and cooperation between the intellectual and the social perspectives. It is for this reason that his answer to the accusation of subjectivism is not objectivism but *inter*subjectivism, just as his answer to the accusation of relativism is not absolutism but humanism. It should be clear that Dewey's humanism is not an individualistic humanism, but itself a thoroughly social or intersubjective humanism—a humanism in which we are fully human only in and through our cooperation, communication, and common, democratic deliberation with others.

5

Pragmatism and Educational Research

In this book we have given an overview of the key ideas of Deweyan pragmatism as they pertain to educational research. One thing that will have become clear, is that pragmatism proposes neither a specific "program" for the conduct of educational research, nor any specific research methods. What it does offer, however, is a distinct perspective on educational research, a specific way to understand the possibilities and limitations of research in, on, and for education. What makes this perspective different from other ways of understanding educational research (and research more generally) is first and foremost its underlying *transactional* framework, which allows for an understanding of knowledge as a function of and for human action, and an understanding of human interaction and communication in thoroughly practical terms. In the preceding chapters we have not only tried to make clear in as much detail as possible what this philosophical view entails for our understanding of knowledge and the process of inquiry; we have also highlighted some of the most important consequences of pragmatism.

(1) Pragmatism provides us with a different way to conceive of the relationship between knowledge and action. From a pragmatist point of view knowledge provides us with possibilities for refining and supporting our day-to-day problem solving, but without a certain foundation for human action. This perspective may influence, for example, the kinds of educational questions that get selected for study.

(2) Pragmatism provides us with a different way to think of the relationship between theory and practice and, more specifically, the relationship

between educational research and educational practice. From a pragmatist point of view it is not that research is theoretical and practice practical and that educational practice is the field of applying the findings of educational research. Both are practices in their own right, with different possibilities and different limitations, and each must inform the other. The relationship between educational research and practice is, in other words, not one of application but of cooperation and coordination. This perspective may influence the ways in which research teams are formed, and who is included in them.

(3) Pragmatism provides us with a different way to think about the objects of our knowledge. It is not that the world of science is closer to reality than the world of everyday life. Objects of knowledge are instruments for action, and different objects, different worlds, provide us with different opportunities and possibilities for action. This perspective may influence, for example, the choice of research methods, emphasizing the use of multiple tools of inquiry to gain different perspectives on the problems at hand.

(4) Finally, pragmatism provides us with a different way to think about objectivity and relativity. It rejects the rigid objectivism that belongs to the tradition of the philosophy of consciousness, the tradition in which it is assumed that there exists an unbridgeable gap between the world of mind and knowledge and the world of matter and action. The alternative to objectivism is, however, not relativism but intersubjectivity; the only world we have, the only world that really matters, so we could say, is our common, intersubjective world, the world in which we live and act together and for which we have a shared responsibility. It is for this reason that the scope of intelligence is not restricted to the domain of means, techniques, and instruments, but includes also the domain of ends, purposes, and values. Dewey's project, after all, was not simply to make human action more scientific but first and foremost to make scientific action more human. This is without doubt an ambitious program—as ambitious today as it was in Dewey's time. This perspective may influence the way in which we regard questions of content in the research we undertake *in relation to* questions about the organization of the context being researched and, for that matter, the researcher's own context.

So, a philosophical examination of pragmatism does not leave the researcher with entirely empty hands. Part of the purpose of this book is precisely to provide *educational* researchers with intellectual resources to rethink and reconsider the point and purpose of their own research activities.

To conclude this book, we want to make some further observations about the insights pragmatism has to offer to some basic questions about educational research.

WHAT IS THE PURPOSE OF EDUCATIONAL RESEARCH?

In some ways, the most important conclusion that follows from a pragmatist understanding of educational research is that educational research is not only about finding better, more sophisticated, more efficient, or effective means for achieving educational ends that are taken for granted, but that inquiry into these very aims, ends, and purposes of education should be an *integral* part of educational research. The "research agenda" for educational research should, in other words, contain both instrumental and value perspectives. Dewey's point, as we showed in chapter 3, was not only that educational research should have a wider remit than simply systematic inquiry into the methods and techniques of education, because that could still result in a split between inquiry into educational means and inquiry into educational ends. Dewey's point was that inquiry into ends, aims, and purposes of education can be nothing but an integral part of inquiry into the means and techniques of education. The point of doing educational research is not only to find out what might be possible or achievable, but also to deal with the question of whether what is possible and achievable is *desirable*—and more specifically whether it is desirable from an educational point of view. We may, for example, well be able to devise highly effective instructional machines. But if this would result in an educational system in which the educational experience of children and young people would simply consist of jumping through the hoops of the instructional machinery, even if they were shown to be successful at promoting certain learning outcomes, we would still *also* need to raise the question of whether what students would learn from the system itself— such as what it demonstrates about what society values about education or what proper learning "is"—is consistent with what we think students ought to learn. In this example, questions of instrumental effectiveness *cannot* be separated from value.

In the same way, Dewey told educational researchers—and educators— not to let themselves be maneuvered into the role of educational technicians; they are not simply adjudicating matters of educational means, while the question of educational ends are decided for them elsewhere.

Dewey provides educators and educational researchers with a compelling set of arguments for why such a restriction is problematic and even dangerously undemocratic.

WHAT CONTRIBUTION CAN EDUCATIONAL RESEARCH MAKE TO EDUCATIONAL PRACTICE?

One of the most significant and characteristic implications of Dewey's transactional approach is that educational research will not result in rules for educational action. Educational research can only ever show us what has been possible in a specific situation—even if that situation was the specific situation of something called a "representative sample"—but it can never tell us once and for all what to do. Educational knowledge, the "product" of educational inquiry, reveals *possible* connections between actions and consequences. Such knowledge is without doubt of extreme importance for educational practitioners, but they should not expect that this will tell them what to do (just as educational researchers should not assume that they have the means for telling practitioners what to do and what not to do).

The reason why the relationship between educational research and educational practice is not one of the simple application of knowledge, is not only to be found in the new way in which pragmatism conceives of knowledge (which is, not as a description of reality but as the relationship between actions and consequences); it also has to do with the fact that the world in which we live is ever-changing and ever-evolving. This means that in a fundamental sense we can never know what the future will bring. Every situation we encounter is in some respect unique. This is not to say that we are continuously empty-handed. Many of our actions are of a habitual nature, and the patterns of action that we have acquired over time do suffice in most instances. Problems only arise in those situations in which our patterns of action do not suffice. Precisely at this point the only way in which we can use the knowledge we have is to direct our observations and inquiries and to suggest possible lines of action. This can help us to understand and deal with the unique situation we are facing, and precisely in this respect it can make our day-to-day problem solving more intelligent. But it is up to educational practitioners to use the outcomes of research in their own practical inquiries and in the judgments involved in their problem solving. This, as we have seen, is why Dewey argues that the final reality of educational science is to be found in the minds of educators (which, in turn, implies that teachers and other educators are not simply passive consumers of educational knowledge, but are as much the creators of educational knowledge, even when they are drawing from research conducted by others, because their very act of problem solving *is* a process of inquiry).

This further means that the improvement of education through educational research cannot be thought of as a process in which educational research provides educational practice with recipes so that educational practice can be "perfected." The problem with such an understanding of the impact of research on practice, and of the idea of improvement more generally, is that it would only make sense if it could be assumed that educational reality itself stays stable over time. This is a highly unlikely assumption for at least three reasons. It is first of all unlikely, because in a fundamental sense, every educational situation is in some respect unique. It is also unlikely because a social practice like education is intrinsically constituted (and reconstituted) through communication and the coordination of action; it depends on the often unpredictable ways in which people act and respond to the actions of others. Finally, it is unlikely that educational reality will remain stable over time for the very practical reason that educators today are confronted with many problems that did not even exist in the past. This suggests that if educational research is to make a contribution to the improvement of education, it will be through the provision of new intellectual and practical resources for the day-to-day problem solving of educators. Improvement of education is, in other words, to be found in the extent to which research enables educators to approach the problems they are faced with in a more intelligent way. This certainly would have implications for the kinds of educational research questions that get framed (and by whom). But it will never result in a perfect educational system.

One could of course argue from a more cynical point of view that one way to reduce the unpredictability of education—and hence the need for educators who are able to approach educational problems in an intelligent way—is to restrict the number of possible actions and activities in educational settings. The perfect example of such an approach can be found in fast-food restaurants. The limited number of items on the menu and the global uniformity of both the preparation of food and the layout of the restaurants restrict both the number of different activities available to those who work in the restaurants, and the number of different actions available to the customers. This makes it easy to order a hamburger all over the world, almost irrespective of whether one knows the local language or not. Since there are hardly any surprises, a limited set of patterns of action, a limited set of habits—or "competencies"—will do in 99.9 percent of all cases. It is clear that such a setup makes intelligent action almost unnecessary. We leave it to the readers to decide to what extent schools in Western countries are moving toward this model, and whether such an approach to the reform and "improvement" of education is desirable, for educational reasons, and on other grounds. It is not within the scope of this book to argue such matters. But a pragmatist understanding of the relationship between knowledge and action and between theory and practice makes such possible consequences visible and explains why they might arise. In educational research settings and others, when questions of "efficiency" get defined and evaluated apart from questions of content and aims, it is a danger that ends will get redefined or circumscribed to fit the most efficient means, rather than vice versa.

WHAT ARE THE LIMITS OF PRAGMATISM AS A PHILOSOPHY?

In this book we have tried to make a case for John Dewey's pragmatism. We believe that it has much to offer, both for wider (philosophical) discussions about the relationship between knowledge and action, the role of science in modern society, questions about objectivity and relativism, and for our understanding of educational research in its relation to educational practice. One of the most interesting lessons that can be learned from Dewey's reconstruction of the history of Western thought is that the disintegrating influence of modern science on everyday life is the result of the fact that the outcomes of modern science have been interpreted with philosophical means that were developed long before modern science emerged. This mismatch has led many people to believe that scientific knowledge only exists for things that are remote from any significant human concern, and that as we approach social and moral questions we must either surrender hope for the guidance of genuine knowledge or, as Dewey put it, "purchase scientific title and authority at the expense of all that is distinctly human" (Dewey 1939b, 51).

Interestingly enough, Dewey's solution to this problem was not to criticize modern science from the outside, but rather to ask what would follow if we would develop our understanding of knowledge on the basis of the worldview of modern science itself. The conclusion—for some, the surprising conclusion—is that if we use the findings of modern science to inform our understanding of science itself, we must abandon the idea that science gives us any privileged access to ultimate reality. If we take science seriously in its own terms (and not in the terms of Greek philosophy), we are forced *not* to take it so seriously; or, to be more precise, we are forced to alter our understanding of science. It then becomes clear that modern science is one human practice among many other significant human practices. Dewey shows, in other words, that if we examine the implications of the content and method of modern science, we end up with anything but the "hegemony" of scientific rationality, but rather with a world full of possibility and potential. In a world still obsessed with the narrow rationality of science, Dewey provided a most effective antidote and a most effective way to reclaim "all that is distinctly human." As we have tried to make clear in this book, Dewey's insight is important not only for the way in which we think generally about science in society, but is especially important for how we understand and approach the field of educational research, in which there have been repeated attempts to make it more narrowly "scientific" without appreciating that the narrow definition of science as a fixed set of methods is one of the most "unscientific" moves of all!

All this is not to suggest that Dewey's pragmatism can solve all the problems of modern life, not in the least because his philosophy—although experimental, open, and genuinely committed to the well-being of all—is in an important sense restricted. Dewey shows us that the natural world, the world of modern science, is a world of human potential and possibility. In doing so, Dewey is able to show that "all that is distinctly human" can have a place in such a world. But there is a price to be paid for this achievement, since the only way in which "all that is distinctly human" can be given a place in the order of being is by redefining it in "naturalistic" terms. After all, the basic model underlying Dewey's writings is that of human beings as living organisms, continuously adapting to an ever-changing environment in which their interaction with other living organisms results in the release of new potentialities, most notably consciousness and self-awareness. Yet this is only one possible way of understanding the world and the place of humans in it, and at the beginning of the twenty-first century we should no longer expect that any one such story, any one metanarrative, can suffice. The catch-22 of Dewey's philosophy, in other words, is that he is able to reveal how open and full of human possibilities the world of modern science actually is—and this is contrary to what many people still are inclined to believe about modern science—yet it still remains the world of modern science.

HOW SHOULD EDUCATIONAL RESEARCHERS "USE" PRAGMATISM?

Our answer to this question is simple, but represents the gist of what this book has been about. Pragmatism is not a recipe for educational research and educational researchers; it does not offer prescriptions. It is, as we have presented it here, as much a way of *un*-thinking certain false dichotomies, certain assumptions, certain traditional practices and ways of doing things, and in this it can open up new possibilities for thought. It is, in short, a resource that can help educational researchers make their research activities more reflective and—to use one of Dewey's most favorite words one final time—more *intelligent*.

Bibliography

Bernstein, R. J. 1983. *Beyond Objectivism and Relativism: Science, Hermeneutics, and Praxis.* Oxford: Basil Blackwell.

———. 1986. *Philosophical Profiles: Essays in a Pragmatic Mode.* Cambridge: Polity Press.

Biesta, G. J. J. 1994. "Education as Practical Intersubjectivity: Towards a Critical-Pragmatic Understanding of Education. *Educational Theory* 44, no. 3: 299–317.

———. 1998. "Mead, Intersubjectivity and Education." *Studies in Philosophy and Education* 17: 73–99.

Boydston, J. A., and K. Poulos, eds. 1978. *Checklist of Writings about John Dewey: 1887–1977.* Second edition, enlarged. Carbondale: Southern Illinois University Press.

Burbules, N. C., B. Warnick, T. McDonough, and S. Johnston. Forthcoming. "The Educational Strand in American Philosophy." In *Blackwell Guide to American Philosophy*, edited by Armen Marsoobian and John Ryder. New York: Blackwell.

Condliffe-Lagemann, E. 2000. *An Elusive Science: The Troubling History of Education Research.* Chicago: University of Chicago Press.

Cook, G. A. 1993. *George Herbert Mead: The Making of a Social Pragmatist.* Urbana: University of Illinois Press.

Coughlan, N. 1975. *Young John Dewey.* Chicago: University of Chicago Press.

Dancy, J. 1985. *An Introduction to Contemporary Epistemology.* Oxford: Blackwell.

Davidson, D. 1980. *Essays on Actions and Events.* Oxford: Clarendon Press.

———. 1984. *Inquiries into Truth and Interpretation.* Oxford: Clarendon Press.

Dewey, J. 1896. "The Reflex Arc Concept in Psychology." In *The Early Works (1882–1898)*, edited by Jo Ann Boydston. Carbondale: Southern Illinois University Press, 5: 96–109.

——. 1899. "Principles of Mental Development as Illustrated in Early Infancy." In *The Middle Works (1899–1924)*, edited by Jo Ann Boydston. Carbondale: Southern Illinois University Press, 1: 175–91.

——. 1903a. "Logical Conditions of a Scientific Treatment of Morality." In *The Middle Works (1899–1924)*, edited by Jo Ann Boydston. Carbondale: Southern Illinois University Press, 3: 3–39.

——. 1903b. *Studies in Logical Theory.* In *The Middle Works (1899–1924)*, edited by Jo Ann Boydston. Carbondale: Southern Illinois University Press, 2: 293–375.

——. 1905. "The Postulate of Immediate Empiricism." In *The Middle Works (1899–1924)*, edited by Jo Ann Boydston. Carbondale: Southern Illinois University Press, 3: 158–67.

——. 1906a. "Beliefs and Existences." In *The Middle Works (1899–1924)*, edited by Jo Ann Boydston. Carbondale: Southern Illinois University Press, 3: 83–100.

——. 1906b. "The Experimental Theory of Knowledge." In *The Middle Works (1899–1924)*, edited by Jo Ann Boydston. Carbondale: Southern Illinois University Press, 3: 107–27.

——. 1907a. "The Control of Ideas by Facts." In *The Middle Works (1899–1924)*, edited by Jo Ann Boydston. Carbondale: Southern Illinois University Press, 4: 78–90.

——. 1907b. "The Intellectualist Criterion for Truth." In *The Middle Works (1899–1924)*, edited by Jo Ann Boydston. Carbondale: Southern Illinois University Press, 4: 50–75.

——. 1908a. "What Pragmatism Means by Practical." In *The Middle Works (1899–1924)*, edited by Jo Ann Boydston. Carbondale: Southern Illinois University Press, 4: 98–115.

——. 1908b. "Does Reality Possess Practical Character?" In *The Middle Works (1899–1924)*, edited by Jo Ann Boydston. Carbondale: Southern Illinois University Press, 4: 125–42.

——. 1909a. *How We Think.* In *The Middle Works (1899–1924)*, edited by Jo Ann Boydston. Carbondale: Southern Illinois University Press, 6: 177–356.

——. 1909b. "The Influence of Darwin on Philosophy." In *The Middle Works (1899–1924)*, edited by Jo Ann Boydston. Carbondale: Southern Illinois University Press, 4: 3–14.

——. 1910. "A Short Catechism Concerning Truth." In *The Middle Works (1899–1924)*, edited by Jo Ann Boydston. Carbondale: Southern Illinois University Press, 6: 3–11.

——. 1911a. "The Problem of Truth." In *The Middle Works (1899–1924)*, edited by Jo Ann Boydston. Carbondale: Southern Illinois University Press, 6: 12–68.

——. 1911b. "A Reply to Royce's Critique." In *The Middle Works (1899–1924)*, edited by Jo Ann Boydston. Carbondale: Southern Illinois University Press, 7: 64–78.

———. 1911c. "Brief Studies in Realism." In *The Middle Works (1899–1924)*, edited by Jo Ann Boydston. Carbondale: Southern Illinois University Press, 6: 103–22.

———. 1912. "Perception and Organic Action." In *The Middle Works (1899–1924)*, edited by Jo Ann Boydston. Carbondale: Southern Illinois University Press, 7: 3–30.

———. 1915a. "The Existence of the World as a Logical Problem." In *The Middle Works (1899–1924)*, edited by Jo Ann Boydston. Carbondale: Southern Illinois University Press, 8: 83–97.

———. 1915b. "The Logic of Judgements of Practice." In *The Middle Works (1899–1924)*, edited by Jo Ann Boydston. Carbondale: Southern Illinois University Press, 8: 14–82.

———. 1916a. *Democracy and Education.* In *The Middle Works (1899–1924)*, Volume 9, edited by Jo Ann Boydston. Carbondale: Southern Illinois University Press.

———. 1916b. "Introduction to *Essays in Experimental Logic*." In *The Middle Works (1899–1924)*, edited by Jo Ann Boydston. Carbondale: Southern Illinois University Press, 10: 320–69.

———. 1917. "The Need for a Recovery of Philosophy." In *The Middle Works (1899–1924)*, edited by Jo Ann Boydston. Carbondale: Southern Illinois University Press, 10: 3–48.

———. 1920. *Reconstruction in Philosophy.* In *The Middle Works (1899–1924)*, edited by Jo Ann Boydston. Carbondale: Southern Illinois University Press, 12: 77–201.

———. 1922a. "Pragmatic America." In *The Middle Works (1899–1924)*, edited by Jo Ann Boydston. Carbondale: Southern Illinois University Press, 13: 306–10.

———. 1922b. *Human Nature and Conduct.* In *The Middle Works (1899–1924)*, Volume 14, edited by Jo Ann Boydston. Carbondale: Southern Illinois University Press.

———. 1922c. "An Analysis of Reflective Thought." In *The Middle Works (1899–1924)*, edited by Jo Ann Boydston. Carbondale: Southern Illinois University Press, 13: 61–71.

———. 1925a. *Experience and Nature.* In *The Later Works (1925–1953)*, Volume 1, edited by Jo Ann Boydston. Carbondale: Southern Illinois University Press.

———. 1925b. "The Development of American Pragmatism." In *The Later Works (1925–1953)*, edited by Jo Ann Boydston. Carbondale: Southern Illinois University Press, 2: 3–21.

———. 1928a. "The Inclusive Philosophical Idea." In *The Later Works (1925–1953)*, edited by Jo Ann Boydston. Carbondale: Southern Illinois University Press, 3: 41–54.

———. 1928b. "Appearing and Appearance." In *The Later Works (1925–1953)*, edited by Jo Ann Boydston. Carbondale: Southern Illinois University Press, 3: 55–73.

———. 1929a. *The Quest for Certainty.* In *The Later Works (1925–1953)*, Volume 4, edited by Jo Ann Boydston. Carbondale: Southern Illinois University Press.

———. 1929b. *The Sources of a Science of Education.* In *The Later Works (1925–1953)*, edited by Jo Ann Boydston. Carbondale: Southern Illinois University Press, 5: 1–40.

———. 1930a. "Conduct and Experience." In *The Later Works (1925–1953)*, edited by Jo Ann Boydston. Carbondale: Southern Illinois University Press, 5: 218–35.

———. 1930b. "From Absolutism to Experimentalism." In *The Later Works (1925–1953)*, edited by Jo Ann Boydston. Carbondale: Southern Illinois University Press, 5: 147–60.

———. 1930c. "Qualitative Thought." In *The Later Works (1925–1953)*, edited by Jo Ann Boydston. Carbondale: Southern Illinois University Press, 5: 243–62.

———. 1931. "Social Science and Social Control." In *The Later Works (1925–1953)*, edited by Jo Ann Boydston. Carbondale: Southern Illinois University Press, 6: 64–68.

———. 1933. *How We Think: A Restatement of the Relation of Reflective Thinking to the Educative Process.* In *The Later Works (1925–1953)*, edited by Jo Ann Boydston. Carbondale: Southern Illinois University Press, 8: 105–352.

———. 1934a. *A Common Faith.* In *The Later Works (1925–1953)*, edited by Jo Ann Boydston. Carbondale: Southern Illinois University Press, 9: 1–58.

———. 1934b. *Art as Experience.* In *The Later Works (1925–1953)*, Volume 10, edited by Jo Ann Boydston. Carbondale: Southern Illinois University Press.

———. 1938a. *Logic: The Theory of Inquiry.* In *The Later Works (1925–1953)*, Volume 12, edited by Jo Ann Boydston. Carbondale: Southern Illinois University Press.

———. 1938b. *Experience and Education.* In *The Later Works (1925–1953)*, edited by Jo Ann Boydston. Carbondale: Southern Illinois University Press, 12: 1–62.

———. 1939a. *Theory of Valuation.* In *The Later Works (1925–1953)*, edited by Jo Ann Boydston. Carbondale: Southern Illinois University Press, 13: 189–252.

———. 1939b. "Experience, Knowledge, and Value: A Rejoinder." In *The Later Works (1925–1953)*, edited by Jo Ann Boydston. Carbondale: Southern Illinois University Press, 14: 3–90.

———. 1941. "Propositions, Warranted Assertibility, and Truth." In *The Later Works (1925–1953)*, edited by Jo Ann Boydston. Carbondale: Southern Illinois University Press, 14: 148–88.

———. 1947. "Liberating the Social Scientist." In *The Later Works (1925–1953)*, edited by Jo Ann Boydston. Carbondale: Southern Illinois University Press, 15: 224–38

———. 1948. "Introduction: Reconstruction as Seen Twenty-Five Years Later." In *The Middle Works (1899–1924)*, edited by Jo Ann Boydston. Carbondale: Southern Illinois University Press, 12: 256–77.

———. 1951. "*How, What,* and *What For* in Social Inquiry." In *The Later Works (1925–1953)*, edited by Jo Ann Boydston. Carbondale: Southern Illinois University Press, 16: 333–42.

Dewey, J., and A. F. Bentley. 1949. *Knowing and the Known.* In *The Later Works (1925–1953)*, edited by Jo Ann Boydston. Carbondale: Southern Illinois University Press, 16: 1–294.

Hickman, L. A. 1990. *John Dewey's Pragmatic Technology.* Bloomington: Indiana University Press.

Horkheimer, M. 1947. *Eclipse of Reason.* New York: Oxford University Press.

Kuklick, B. 1985. *Churchmen and Philosophers: From Jonathan Edwards to John Dewey.* New Haven: Yale University Press.

Langfeld, H. S. 1943. "Jubilee of the Psychological Review: Fifty Volumes of the Psychological Review." *Psychological Review* 50: 143–55.

Leahey, Th. H. 1987. *A History of Psychology.* Englewood Cliffs, N.J.: Prentice-Hall.

Lovejoy, A. O. 1963. *The Thirteen Pragmatisms and Other Essays.* Baltimore, Md.: The Johns Hopkins Press.

Peirce, Ch. S. 1955. *Philosophical Writings.* New York: Dover.

Phillips, D. C., and N. C. Burbules. 2000. *Postpositivism and Educational Research.* Lanham, Md.: Rowman & Littlefield.

Putnam, H. 1990. *Realism with a Human Face.* Cambridge, Mass.: Harvard University Press.

———. 1995. *Pragmatism.* Oxford: Blackwell.

Quine, W. V. O. 1980. *From a Logical Point of View: Nine Logico-Philosophical Essays.* Second edition, revised. Cambridge, Mass.: Harvard University Press.

Rajchman, J, and C. West. 1985. *Post-analytic Philosophy.* New York: Columbia University Press.

Rorty, R. 1980. *Philosophy and the Mirror of Nature.* Oxford: Blackwell.

———. 1982. *Consequences of Pragmatism.* Brighton: Harvester Press.

Russell, B. 1922. "As a European Radical Sees It." *Freeman* 4: 608–10.

———. 1940. *An Inquiry into Meaning and Truth.* New York: W. W. Norton.

Schneider, H. W. 1963. *A History of American Philosophy.* New York: Columbia University Press.

Sleeper, R. W. 1986. *The Necessity of Pragmatism: John Dewey's Conception of Philosophy.* New Haven, Conn.: Yale University Press.

Stenhouse, L. 1983. *Authority, Education and Emancipation.* London: Heinemann Educational Books.

Thayer, H. S. 1973. *Meaning and Action: A Critical History of Pragmatism.* Indianapolis, Ind.: Bobbs-Merrill.

Titchener, E. B. 1898. "The Postulates of Structural Psychology." *The Psycho-logical Review* 5: 449–65.

Welchman, J. 1989. "From Absolute Idealism to Instrumentalism: The Problem of Dewey's Early Philosophy." *Transactions of the Charles S. Peirce Society* 25: 407–19.

Index

About the Authors

Gert J. J. Biesta is professor of educational theory at the School of Education and Lifelong Learning of the University of Exeter in England and visiting professor for education and democratic citizenship at the Department of Education of Örebro University in Sweden. He is editor in chief of the journal *Studies in Philosophy of Education*. He has authored, coauthored, or edited nine books and has published numerous articles and book chapters on educational theory and the philosophy of educational research. He takes his main inspiration from pragmatism (Dewey, Mead) and poststructuralism (Derrida, Levinas). His work has been published in English, Dutch, German, and Swedish. His recent books include *Derrida & Education* (coedited with Denise Egéa-Kuehne, 2001) and *Pedagogisch bekeken. De rol van pedagogische idealen in de onderwijspraktijk* [From an educational point of view. The role of educational ideals in teaching] (written with Fred Korthagen and Hildelien Verkuyl, 2002). His Dutch translation of Dewey's *Experience and Education* (with Siebren Miedema) was published in 1999. He has given seminars on the issues related to this book in England, Switzerland, and Sweden and has benefited tremendously from the opportunity to discuss his ideas about pragmatism and educational research with students and colleagues in these different countries.

Nicholas C. Burbules is Grayce Wicall Gauthier Professor in the Department of Educational Policy Studies at the University of Illinois, Urbana–Champaign. He has published widely in the areas of philosophy of education, technology and education, and critical social and political theory. He is also the current editor of *Educational Theory*. His most recent books include: *Watch IT: The Promises and Risks of New Information Technologies for Education* (with Thomas A. Callister Jr., 2000); in this series, *Postpositivism and Educational Research* (with D. C. Phillips, 2000); and *Globalization and Education: Critical Perspectives* (coedited with Carlos Torres, 2000).